Teach Yourself to

WIN

Cy Young Winner Steve Stone Tells What It Takes to Make Success a Habit

Steve Stone
with
Nolan Anglum

Bonus Books, Inc., Chicago

95 94 93 92 91   5 4 3 2 1

Library of Congress Catalog Card Number: 91-70964

International Standard Book Number: 0-929387-54-6

Bonus Books, Inc.
160 East Illinois Street
Chicago, Illinois 60611

First Edition

Printed in the United States of America

For Dorothy Stone, my mother

Contents

At Odds with Earl

"Steve, the book on you is you're a loser, that you've always been a loser, you're a loser now, and, if you ask me, there's a good chance you'll always be a loser."

Earl Weaver, manager of the Baltimore Orioles, pulled no punches in Oakland during the All-Star break of 1979. The team was doing great. They were on the verge of running away with the American League East. They had a star pitching lineup and were one of the winningest teams in baseball history. By contrast, at mid-season, I was 6–7 (73–79 lifetime).

"Earl," I argued, "what the book doesn't say is that I've always played for teams that were sub-.500. I'm not a dominating pitcher so I will pitch to the approximate performance of my team. What do you want from me?" I was furious. The argument was all too familiar. Earl and I had been doing battle for months, but this time, it was obvious, that one of us was going to win the war.

Earl leaned across the desk that separated us. Our pitching coach, Ray Miller, who had called this meeting, sat off to the side of his own desk like a referee. From my vantage, I could see the other players in the locker room eyeing us through the glass windows which enclosed Earl's office.

Earl had a habit of pointing when he wanted to get his point across, and it was only a matter of seconds before he had his nicotine-stained finger right in my face. "Let me tell you how baseball works. I've got you over here as my fifth starter. If next year I can find somebody who can do your job better than you, then I'll trade you and you can be whatever you will be somewhere else. But, if I can't find somebody to do your job better than you, then you will be back with the Orioles in 1980."

The more excited Earl got, the louder he became. His voice, gravelly from years of smoking, sounded like fingernails across a blackboard as he shoved his face right into mine. From the beginning, Earl and I had a rocky relationship, but, at that moment, I considered him the most disgusting human being I had ever encountered in my entire life.

"I'm going to give you two starts after the All-Star Game," he sneered, "then I will evaluate. In September, I'm going to a three-man starting rotation. If you're one of the best three, then you'll pitch. If you're not, then you won't." From the self-satisfied look on his face, I could read the pleasure he got from giving me the ultimatum.

"That's real good, Earl," I leaned back in my chair, trying to make myself as calm as Earl was heated up, enjoying the arrogance that must have

♦

shown in my expression. "You've got a potential Cy Young Award winner in Mike Flanagan, so he'll be one of the three for sure. There's Jim Palmer, a three-time Cy Young Award winner, who you think is your son, so there's number two. Then there's Scott McGregor, one of the finest young left-handers in the league. Toss in Dennis Martinez, who you think is going to be the next Jim Palmer. Now just where does that leave me?"

Earl eased off, letting the smug expression on his face tell me he could care less. "I don't know where that leaves you, but I do know that you've got two starts after the All-Star break."

With his arms folded across his chest, I could tell Earl was ready for more, expecting me to jump right back at him as I had already done dozens of times that season. Next to baseball, arguing was Earl's favorite sport. Instead of giving him the satisfaction of shouting back, though, I got up, nodded to Ray, gave Earl one last look of total disgust, and left without saying a word. I quietly shut the office door behind me. Just as I knew it would, my silence enraged Earl even more.

Earl shot up, throwing back his chair in the process. "I'm not through," he screamed. I walked slowly across the locker room, daring Earl to follow me. Those teammates who were there stopped what they were doing and turned to watch the show.

By this time, I had learned Earl's timing. I passed my locker and kept right on toward the door, giving Earl enough time to get out of the office and into the locker room. "Two starts," I heard him yell from behind me. Without seeing him, I knew he had his arm stuck straight out and his finger directed at me. "Two starts."

I had come to the Orioles in 1979 at a time when the first thing they needed was a good outfielder, preferably batting .300, and the last thing they needed was another pitcher. I was a relatively high-

♦

3

priced free agent, although my salary of $182,000 a year would be dwarfed by today's standards, and I was given a four-year contract, almost unheard of for a middle-of-the-road pitcher who had never won twenty games.

For that kind of money, the Baltimore fans expected a superman, and to beat the pitching staff already in the Oriole organization, it would have taken one. Sports fans all over the world waste no time in giving their favorite team advice, but baseball fans go beyond that. There is a special relationship between a baseball team and its city, much like a marriage, where love, hate, loyalty, pride and criticism are the ties that bind. Not a day went by in which I didn't get press, mostly negative.

Even the Orioles players weren't behind me. Before I even signed my contract, I was met with an article in the *Baltimore Sun* in which Jim Palmer let it be known just what he thought of the organization signing another pitcher, an injured one to boot. And it wasn't good. To make matters even worse, I was making almost as much as he was. Palmer had signed a long-term contract with the Orioles for about $200,000 a year. At the time, star pitchers were making double that or more. He had traded megabucks for security. His choice, but I could understand how he felt.

The team may have been on a roll, but, for me, things were going downhill fast in Baltmore in the middle of 1979.

Suddenly I was faced with the fact that my role with the Baltimore Orioles didn't revolve around the three and a half years I had left on my contract. It revolved around two starts, and if my win-a-few-lose-a-few calculations were accurate, I was due for a couple of bad games.

I was angry and hurt, but most of all I was frustrated. To say my ego had been bruised was an

♦
4

understatement. Despite my arrogant bravado, I knew Earl was as good as his word. If, in September, I was not one of the top three pitchers for the Orioles, I would be whatever I would be, somewhere else. As I walked away from the locker room that day, all I could think of was how to salvage my career, not my job, but my career.

First and foremost, I thought of myself as a baseball player. Sure, I was a son, a brother, a restauranteur, a friend, but those things came second to the thrill of standing on the mound. From the time I was six, there were only two seasons, the baseball season and the rest of the year when I waited for the baseball season to come around again. My life revolved around the bat, the ball, and the glove. Every major goal in my life revolved around baseball. Now, after eleven years of professional baseball, Earl Weaver threatened to take me out of the game, and there wasn't a doubt in my mind he would take great pleasure in doing so.

When I was seventeen, my father took me to Cleveland Stadium to watch the Indians play the Washington Senators. At that time, fans could gather in the stands behind the bullpen. I remember watching Pete Richert, a talented left-handed pitcher, as he warmed up. He threw the ball so hard it seemed to explode in the catcher's glove and his curveball was better than anything I ever dreamed of throwing. I studied him for the longest time, wishing I could be even half as good a pitcher as he was. By the time the game started and Richert was on the mound, I was convinced there was no way any batter would get a hit off him. That day Cleveland killed him, knocking him out in the second inning. I thought, "If Richert wasn't good enough, what does it take to win in the major leagues?" That same question began to haunt me again.

I had spent my career vascillating between the belief that I belonged in the majors and doubting my ability to stay there. In college, I was plagued with

◆

Thurman Munson as a teammate. Plagued because Thurman was so talented that I lost perspective on my own game by comparison. As a professional, I never stood out among the true greats in the game. I allowed the expectations of others to determine my own performance. Every team I had ever played for was middle-of-the-road. I fit right in. I'm not saying I agreed with every manager's use of me, but up until now, no one had questioned my ability. What was Earl's problem? Bill Veeck knew what he was getting when he hired me for the White Sox, the team I had been with before the Orioles.

My first start after the All-Star break was against the Oakland A's. There wasn't a doubt in my mind that I *could* win, I had beaten Oakland before, but that was no guarantee that I could go out against the A's and win *this* time. After all, my limitations were complicated by some pretty severe emotional conditions. And what I needed was that guarantee.

During the next week, I did more soul-searching and personal evaluation than I had ever done in my life. I had been unhappy since I arrived in Baltimore, certainly, but more than that, I knew that I had never gotten the most out of my ability. There were times of brilliance in my career; however, these were more than offset by those times when my performance was mediocre, just enough to get by. I knew there was a winner inside me, the problem was I didn't know how to get it out. I had attributed the good times as much to luck as skill and took the bad times in stride, knowing that sooner or later my luck would change and I'd be on a winning streak again. However, in the light of some honest assessment, it was apparent, even to me, that I had been using this "due for a good one, due for a bad one" philosophy as an excuse for my own shortcomings. And if that were true, I didn't need luck to win against Oakland, all I needed was skill.

♦

I took inventory. I had to assume I was no more or less prepared to play than anyone else on the field. At a little over five feet nine inches, I was smaller than most of the other pitchers in the league, and, by this time, had suffered enough injuries that I wasn't over-powering. My only advantage, as I saw it, was to be more mentally prepared to play than anyone else. The problem was, how to become that way.

Like many other people, I had read books on positive thinking, creative visualization, meditation. I had even dabbled in hypnosis. The books I had read were fine, to a point. While the concepts intrigued me, I was not about to dedicate years of my life to reach a level of consciousness only vaguely defined by the authors. Not one of them presented a practical enough method for me to use in my everyday life, so I pretty much ignored them. However, I am a realist, and I knew that my past readings were the best place to start. I didn't have eighteen months to turn my life around. I had one week. I wasn't searching for nir-vana, I wanted to win two ball games. Somehow I had to sift through this swamp of information, condense it, and mold it into a usable technique for success. I decided to start at the beginning.

I sat down with a piece of paper and made a list of all the reasons why I wasn't successful, my limitations. Earl Weaver didn't understand me, never had used me properly, expected me to pitch with varying layoffs between games, had unreasonable expectations of my performance, and he'd been on my back since I joined the team. My rotator cuff injury in 1976 had never healed properly. The Baltimore fans were not on my side from the start. My teammates treated me as an outsider. I missed my home in Chicago. The ballpark was made for hitters, not pitchers. My shoulder hurt and the doctors were no help. And there was more.

After an hour, I realized I was filling up the page at profuse proportions. I stopped and looked at all the things I had written. I read over the page again, and then a third time. I read aloud what I had written. I listened to myself as I said "Earl Weaver . . . ," "Jim Palmer . . . ," "My landlord . . . ," "The *Baltimore Sun* . . . ," "The fans. . . ." I must have read the paper ten times before I figured out that every problem on that list was someone else's fault. I had accepted responsibility for nothing. For the first time it dawned on me, as if in bright letters, what these things really were. RATIONALIZATIONS. These weren't reasons not to succeed, they were excuses for failure. It was then I realized that the only reason I hadn't been successful up to this point was ME.

I sat back for a moment. The truth is the hardest thing to face, especially if it is an unpleasant truth about yourself. Times in the past when I had failed came back to me. It was as if someone were replaying parts of my life in slow motion. I made myself relive those moments and watched as I shifted the responsibility of my own failure to someone or something else. Not once, not twice, but in every case where I had not succeeded, I discovered I had placed the blame every place but where it belonged. I took a deep breath and admitted that Earl Weaver was right, I wasn't the quality of pitcher that should have been out there for Baltimore. Most of all, I wasn't the quality of pitcher I wanted to be for myself.

At that point I had some hard questions to answer. What was I going to do to wipe away the rationalizations and start to perform? What kind of system could I use to finally get out of myself what I wanted to get out of myself? What can I do against Oakland to win? I went back to the books I had read.

I remembered reading that the only true limitations are the physical ones, and even those aren't overwhelming. We all know of athletes who excel despite physical handicaps. Monty Stratton is a good example. Beethoven composed some of the world's

♦

finest music and he was deaf. Franklin Delano Roosevelt led the United States out of a depression and through a World War and he was confined to a wheelchair. So what were my limitations? I reviewed my list again. Comparatively, I had none.

Up until mid-1979 I was a good enough pitcher to earn a paycheck, but not good enough to live up to my own personal expectations. That was about to change. Despite what Earl Weaver said, despite my performance in the past, at that moment I knew I could be the best pitcher on the Oriole team. I ripped up the page of excuses. They were no longer valid limitations on my performance.

Right then, I determined that it didn't matter what other people thought I was or what I should be. It didn't matter what they wanted out of me. All that mattered was that I satisfy my own personal goal. It didn't take but a moment for me to realize what it was. I wrote it down:

My goal is to make myself the best pitcher in the major leagues.

Lofty task for a guy who was six games under break even and the fifth starter on one of the most respected pitching staffs in either league. I was playing with the best of the best, sure Hall-of-Famers. I was no longer a young player with years ahead of me to prove myself. Behind me was a career of inconsistency and lackluster performance, and my manager was convinced I was a loser. But none of that was important any longer. I threw away the paper with the rationalizations.

I had always felt that if I won two games, I was due for a bad one. I realized that there is no such thing as due for a bad one. And I didn't have a three and a half year contract with the Baltimore Orioles anymore, I had two starts. If I were ever going to make it happen, I had to make it happen right then.

2

Zero In on the Negatives

Your worst enemies could very well be your family, friends, and co-workers. Frightening thought, isn't it? The unfortunate truth of the matter, though, is that those closest to us carry the most influence on our behavior and this daily intimacy can be the most effective weapon against us.

Consider this. Bright and early Monday morning you arrive at work. The traffic was light on the drive in and the deep blue sky and gentle breeze promise a great day. You're feeling good and already you've planned most of the morning, knowing it's going to be a productive one. You go for a cup of coffee and run into Fred. "Beautiful day," you say. Fred responds,

"For a Monday." "Right," you say, and by the time you get back to your desk, just a little bit of your energy has been drained.

Now, I'm not saying Fred was in a bad mood when he said "For a Monday," because he probably wasn't. But without realizing it, Fred just set the tone for the rest of your day, and it was a negative one. What's worse, you allowed him to do it. And you consider Fred to be one of your friends.

Pretty simplistic example, I know, but one which illustrates how profoundly those around us affect our lives, some of the time without our even realizing it.

As I said before, from the time I was able to hold a bat and throw a ball, baseball was my life. However, in the fifth grade, there was a music teacher who convinced me that what I really wanted to do was play the clarinet. How did she do that? Simple, she got up in front of the class and explained what a wonderful thing the ability to play music was, and as I listened, her love of music and appreciation for the instrument infected me. By the time she was through, I wanted to be Benny Goodman.

That night, I brought the clarinet home. My parents politely listened as I attempted to make music. In the days that followed, I diligently practiced enough so I could make "Mary Had a Little Lamb" decipherable. Meanwhile, my friends and classmates proved to be less understanding. Rather than accept my squeaking as a natural part of the learning process, they teased me, telling me that I'd never be able to play.

What the teacher had made look so easy, I found difficult. Where she had made music, I only made noise. Being a clarinet player was beginning to look out of my grasp, and I was not used to failing. So, after three weeks, I bought into my friends' opinion and gave up the clarinet. They were right, I'd never learn how to play.

♦

11

"I can't do it," I said to the teacher when I returned the clarinet.

"Oh yes, you can," she said. "You just don't want to."

"No, I can't." I put the clarinet on her desk and left the classroom, absolutely convinced she was wrong. Me a musician! No way.

Many years later, I realized who was really wrong.

Granted, not being able to play the clarinet has been inconsequential in my life, but, in retrospect, I wonder how many other things, maybe not so insignificant, I have not been able to do because I was convinced I couldn't. And you could ask yourself the same question.

Don't get me wrong, I loved playing baseball; but after my failure at the clarinet, baseball also provided safe haven. Throughout my school years, I progressed from Little League to our high school team, a success all the way. People around me, friends and family, supported my efforts, and why not? When a child clearly excels at an activity, the natural thing to do is encourage even more effort. No one, including myself, doubted that I had a bright future ahead of me in the game. However, one has to ask oneself, does success in one field of endeavor mask failure in another? At the time, I wouldn't have known, because my complete focus—mental, physical and emotional—was on the game.

It was sort of disguising the negative with a positive. Since I played ball so well, why bother with other things?After all, there was nothing I could do as well. I made little effort to diversify. All my needs, that of success, of support and of reward were fulfilled on the field. And the barriers were going up.

Negatives in our lives are sometimes insidious; they creep up on us without our realizing it. The barriers to my playing the clarinet were obvious. I was used to instant success, and with music that success

♦

was not there. I was supported by those around me in baseball; with the clarinet that was not the case. As a matter of fact, most of my friends made a joke of it. And even my parents, who never said, "Don't do it," didn't give me the same support as they had with baseball. So the negative of quitting was met with the positive of returning to guaranteed success. It was the comfort of guaranteed success that stopped me cold.

We all do it, hide in those things in which we feel comfortable. How many of you don't dance because you don't know how? Little thing. Besides, you've gotten this far without taking a turn on the floor, why start now?

How many of you don't swim? A more important thing. If you can't, you've spent your whole life avoiding situations where being able to hold your own in water is necessary. If you're lucky, you can spend the rest of your life doing the same thing. Maybe you don't look so good in a suit anymore. Even more reason not to try.

What about going back to school? A big thing. But high school was a drag and you didn't do that well in it anyway. Besides, you have a good enough job. So what if you could use a little more money, you've made do so far. And everybody could use a little more money. If you made more, you'd only spend more. Only young kids go to school. You can't spare the time.

Okay, so we've covered a couple of topics that a number of us are faced with. Plus, we're all in agreement with why we don't do anything about them. You'd be hard pressed to find anybody to admit to having extra time on their hands. Your family would prefer you at home, anyway. You've got plenty of support for your position. So where's the negative?

The negative is that you've accomplished nothing because you've convinced yourself you can't. The seed to dance, swim, or return to school must have

♦

been planted in your mind—you thought of doing it. Your wife hasn't complained about your not dancing with her in years; you stay fully dressed on the beach (never having to worry about sunburn); and you're home every night, most of the time watching TV. These seeds have been killed both by your negative beliefs about yourself and the support of those negatives from those around you.

And then there are times when we overcome the negatives. As I said, baseball consumed my life, to the expense of my social life, my family and school. Not that I was ever in danger of failing, but my academic performance in high school was secondary to baseball. I assumed that my ability to play would carry me from high school to college to the majors. My teammates and coaches never disagreed; however, during my senior year a guidance counselor threw me for a loop. She took one look at my transcript and suggested that I skip college and join the army.

"Are you crazy? Nobody is picked up for the majors from the army," I told her.

She shook her head, "With these grades, you can hardly be considered college material."

"I'm not interested in being college material," I said, "I want to play ball." When you're young, your perspective is sometimes skewed. Despite her recommendation, I knew I'd be going to college.

So why was this negative ignored?

Part of it was my desire *not* to join the army. Part of it was the support of my family and friends with respect to my baseball career. And part of it was the fact that I had been so conditioned to my plan of high school, college, majors that I was not prepared in a fifteen minute counseling session to give it up. But the primary reason that this woman's advice was ignored was my overwhelming belief, my unshakable goal, that I was destined to play ball. I believed so strongly in this that I don't think anything could have swayed me. Not the fact that I wasn't a good student. Not the fact that scholarship offers, athletic or academic, were not rolling in. Not the fact that I was up against a higher level of competitor than I had ever been. No, I was firm in my goal to make it to the major league level. Nothing could have driven me from this course. Not even Thurman Munson, and there was a negative input if I ever saw one.

I was in Columbus, on the campus of the Ohio State University, having made the 1965 high school All-State team. I was primed and wanted to go to Ohio State. Right off, the school staff let me know that they wouldn't be offering me a scholarship since they had all the pitchers they could use. So there I was, turned down before I even started, when Thurman Munson walked into my life.

The Ohio All-State program divided the state into East and West divisions and Thurman and I wound up on the East team, me as a pitcher and Thurman as a shortstop. Also on the Ohio All-State East team that year were a couple of other players who later made it into the major leagues, Larry Hisle playing center field and Gene Tenace at third base. It was one great All-State team that year to say the least.

Although he had already made a name for himself catching, at that point, Thurman wasn't interested in being a catcher. As a matter of fact, at that point in time, Thurman wasn't interested in doing much of anything other than what Thurman wanted to do. Not a real likable fellow. At any rate, he went head to head for the shortstop position with a guy I knew from the Cleveland area named Jimmy Redman. I knew Redman from a summer league team and knew he was good. What a shock it must have been for Thurman when Redman beat him out for shortstop for the opening game. It was obvious that Thurman was not a person who was used to losing. Even as a high school player, Thurman was something special, not only in his natural talent, but in his determination. The next game, Thurman was the starting shortstop.

I was more fortunate. I was the starting pitcher for the opening game and the Ohio All-State East team went on to win the three-game series against the West.

In later years, while Thurman and I were both at Kent State and Redman was at Western Michigan, I was always able to get a rise out of Thurman by the sheer mention of Jimmy Redman's name. Even after we had both made it to the major leagues, Thurman took great delight in the fact that he had made it to the top while Redman only got to Triple A ball in the White Sox system and then wound up playing for a year or so in Japan. When Thurman Munson set his mind to it, every competition was a life or death situation.

It was obvious to me, and to just about everyone else at O.S.U. that year, that Thurman Munson was destined for a great career in pro ball. He was my roommate for road games, and over the course of the camp I came to know him better. While he was a fearsome competitor, I saw that he was also a gentle, caring man. I spent a great many nights on the road listening to how difficult it was to be away from his girlfriend in Canton, Ohio. It came as no surprise to me when Diane later became his wife.

While I was learning to like Thurman better personally, as far as baseball was concerned, he was intimidating. His natural talent put him head and shoulders above just about everyone else, especially me, who was still smaller than most of the other players around. When recruiters came, I knew they were coming to look at Thurman. Local sportswriters came to write about Thurman. Throughout my career I had always held my own against the talents of my teammates; however, this was the first time I felt that someone else's ability at the game could affect my

♦

future. I don't know how his popularity affected the others on the team, but I sure felt like I was living in the shadow his image had created. Any other year there might not have been such a dominating player. I can tell you I felt a little bit cheated that there happened to be a player of Thurman's caliber on the All-State team the same year I was chosen.

Even with my good showing at camp, scholarship offers still did not come rolling in, so by the end of camp I had decided to go to Kent State. Kent was not my first preference, but it was a good school, nonetheless. I wanted otherwise, but had accepted my only real option. I was even beginning to see the positives. What a shock it was when Thurman said, "Kent State! I'm going to be your catcher." I felt a black cloud forming over my head.

"Catcher?" I managed, "but you're a shortstop now."

"No, no," Thurman said, "I'm a catcher, but I just didn't want to catch here. So it looks like we're going to spend four more years together." I can still see the grin on his face.

Four more years of being overshadowed by Thurman Munson, I thought. That black cloud became a thunderstorm. Already the negatives were setting in.

As you have probably put together by now, Thurman Munson was his own man, right or not. During the All-State tournament, he chose his position, and at Kent State he started off by bucking the varsity baseball coach's rule regarding batting practice.

At that time the batting cage was indoors underneath the stands in the gymnasium. The rule was nobody could throw batting practice or hit without a football helmet on. The helmets were the old fashioned kind, cardboard and bulky, and Thurman refused to wear one. We were just freshman players with no clout, not even involved with the varsity, but Thurman flat refused. It even got to the point where

♦

the freshman coach, Bud Middaugh, was called in to talk to the varsity coach, Moose Paskert. To no avail, Thurman Munson, high school star or not, was going to wear a helmet or he was not going in the cage.

Time passed, and Thurman was not getting the practice even he realized he needed. I know it just about killed him when he finally donned the helmet and walked into the cage. The coach may have gotten the helmet on, but Thurman felt it was his obligation to continue to gripe. Like I said, he was not a gracious loser. Another life or death situation for Thurman, but little did he realize how life or death it would turn out to be.

He was throwing batting practice to our shortstop his second or third time out. Things were going along pretty well, when all of a sudden, this kid lines one right off Thurman's forehead and knocks him cold, even with the helmet. Thurman hit the floor like a sack of cement. Who knows what would have happened if he hadn't had the helmet on. Needless to say, Thurman never gave anyone an argument about the helmet again. But it took one helluva knock in the head to get Thurman to back down.

While Thurman's baseball career was taking off, what seemed to me, effortlessly, I was working morning to night. Thurman Munson drew a lot of attention to the Kent State team and there seemed to always be scouts, writers, and coaches in the bleachers sizing him up. I was beginning to feel like I was never going to get my chance to show what I could do. After all, everyone was there to see Thurman. That's what I had convinced myself of, anyway.

And it was true. Just about everyone was there to see Thurman. But the negative belief system that I had built for myself did not allow me to realize that, even though they were there to see Thurman, there was no way they were going to be able to see Thurman without seeing me. Thurman may have been the price

◆

of admission, but I had forgotten I was part of the show. Time had given me an appreciation of Thurman Munson, and I considered him a friend, but I made him an obstacle to my own success.

If I had a bad game, I passed it off. What did it matter anyway? Thurman was who they were interested in. I blamed the attention *he* was given, for the lack of attention *I* generated. The way I had it figured, I could still have a career in pro ball, I just had to wait until Thurman got out of the way for them to see me.

Does this sound familiar to you? It should because we all have a Thurman Munson in our lives. Maybe it was the "genius" who followed you through school, always making you number two to his or her number one. Or it could be the guy in the next office who always seems to have the better idea. Or maybe it's just your Saturday golf partner who can make a twenty-foot putt, time after time, while your ball always ends up a few inches short of the cup. With people like that haunting us, it's easy to stop putting forth that extra effort. What's the difference? They're going to beat you out every time.

With that kind of a negative attitude, they sure are. When we believe we will fail, we will. Not only will we fail, there comes a point when we quit trying. Do this enough times and this negative attitude about what we cannot do controls our lives. And when we quit trying, we quit living.

I am reminded of a friend of mine who played ball with me in college. He had not been drafted by a major league team, but I knew him to be a fairly decent athlete. I was in Ohio just before spring training one year and ran into him. We had dinner.

He spent the whole evening talking about only needing a chance. He would have played better ball in school, but the coach didn't give him a chance, preferring to play the "stars" of the team. He would have been drafted but didn't have a chance to be seen. He could have been picked up by one of the farm clubs, but nobody gave him a chance to show what he could do. He got to me. I told him to meet me in Arizona, I'd see he got his chance.

A few days later, I left for Arizona expecting my friend to meet me the following week. I spoke to the staff and they were willing to take a look. He called me to let me know he would be there. "Wednesday, Steve, I'll be there on Wednesday."

On Tuesday I got a call. He just couldn't get away right then. He needed a few more days. "The weekend, Steve, I'll be there over the weekend." The weekend came and went, then it was "Friday, Steve, I'll be there on Friday."

If you guessed that he never did show up, you're right. And why didn't he? He was getting his chance. Wasn't that what he wanted? At the time I thought so, but now I know different.

His not getting a chance was the excuse for his failure and my opening the door for him would take away this excuse. The negatives had so firmly been cemented in his mind concerning his ability to play ball, that he had convinced himself he never would be able to make it to the major leagues. If he didn't show up in Arizona, he would never have to face that fact. He could always blame someone else. If he never tried, he never failed.

What's even sadder, to this day, he still dreams about what he could have done if he had only been given the chance.

"If only's" are the most devastating kinds of failures, primarily because they occur because of self-imposed limitations. "If only" I had been given that promotion, then the boss would know what I could do. "If only" I could have made it to the tryouts, I would have made the team. "If only" life were fair, then I would have my due. "If only." "If only."

♦

The reality is that "if only" we had passed on the negatives and focused on the positives, we would have had those opportunities we feel we lost, and more.

"If only" the promotion had come your way. What about showing what you can do on a daily basis? No, you don't try because you feel that the boss wouldn't give you the proper credit. Or no one would pay attention. Or you might not succeed and then your situation would be worse. You might have even gotten that promotion, and then what would you have done? What would happen if you failed then?

Sound silly? Or familiar?

Where do these fears, these negatives in our lives, come from? Simple, they come from ourselves, built from little bits of data supplied by those around us. No, not remarks that say "You will never succeed because you are *whatever*." These are recognizable and easy to combat with intelligence and a bit of anger. The dangerous negatives are the ones subtly placed in our subconscious.

"I don't want to try out for the school play. Mary always gets the lead anyway."

"Why knock myself out? They only promote guys with a college degree."

"I like myself overweight. Besides, there's no diet in the world that's going to work in the long run."

Do you see what we do? Not only do we justify our failures by these negative excuses, we rationalize our lack of effort by them, too. And we *all* do it. It's as natural as breathing. So natural, in fact, that we usually don't recognize that we're being defeated by ourselves. What's worse, over time, those around us begin to support our excuses. There's always the spouse who would prefer you to stay home. Or the co-worker who prefers you maintain the status quo. Or the parent who wants you to take the safe route. All of them with good intentions.

♦
21

So how do you recognize these negatives and begin to fight them? That's tougher than you think because they're all around you.

The first thing you've got to do is determine what it is you *really* want. I wanted the major leagues. I was determined to play professional baseball. Do you want that promotion? Or do you want something else? Whatever it is, I'm here to tell you that you can have it. All you've got to do is recognize what's stopping you.

So, what's your goal? It doesn't have to be something like a promotion or money or power. Perhaps you would like to be a better parent. Or maybe it's time you went back to school to learn all those things you always were curious about. Maybe you'd like to be happier in your life. Does the clarinet interest you? Anything can be a goal.

Pick one, or two, or three. There are no limits. *Write them down.* Use the paper as a bookmark, so each time you open this book you are reminded of what it is that you want. If you think of another one as you go on, add it to the list. Forget about how outrageous they seem. No one has to see the list but you. The more you add, the greater your chances are of achieving them. Do you know why? Because as you expand your dreams, you increase your belief that they are achievable. The positives start to overcome the negatives. Only then do we develop the inner courage to remove the negatives from our lives.

So the day will come when you greet Fred with a cheerful "Good morning" and he'll automatically respond "For a Monday"; and instead of agreeing with him, letting his negatives influence you, you'll fight back and say "For any day. Because something great is going to happen."

3

Blockades to Success

Now that you've got your list of goals we can talk about achieving them. The first one . . . Wait, you say, I can't do that. Why not? Now you start with the list of blockades to your success. I'm too young. Too old. I don't have a college degree. I don't have time. And you go on. And on. Go ahead, I've got time. But when you've finished, we're going to look at these hinderances and really evaluate what they are.

There are two kinds of blockades to success, the ones that are really there and the ones that are there only because you think they are. To start we'll take the easy ones, the real ones, the ones we can identify.

Real impediments to success tend toward the physical. The likelihood of someone making a major league team in his eighties is nil. Just as a person with no legs will not make the Olympic skating team. And a person who is tone deaf will never sing at the Met. Goals set with real blockades in the way are not goals, they are dreams, fantasies, that will never be fulfilled. While dreams are wonderful things, they must not be mistaken for goals. To do this would be to create a convenient reinforcement for failure. Then the blockade ceases to be real and becomes imagined.

But let's get on with some real blockades that may not seem so absurd. I can't be made office manager because the rules say only those with a college degree can be promoted. We'll never get that new house because it just costs too much money. I'll never learn to play the piano because it just takes too much time. I'd love to coach the little league team, but I just don't play ball that well. Or like my friend who never showed up at spring training in Arizona, I couldn't come down and try out because I just couldn't get away.

Do these sound like real blockades to you? They don't to me. While real blockades do exist, they are few when goals are truly goals. Most of the blockades to our success are our own, built from the negative belief systems that have crept into our minds.

Rick Sutcliffe won the Cy Young Award in 1984. He was a wonderful pitcher the Cubs got in a trade from the Cleveland Indians in 1984. He went 16–1 for the National League East Champions, and ended up 20–6 for the season. Rick, a fastball pitcher, signed with the Cubs in the off-season for $1.9 million per year. But in 1985, he got hurt. Although he gave proper attention to his injuries, his game suffered through the balance of 1985 and 1986. No matter what he did, Rick could not bring the level of his

♦

performance back to his 1984 standard. His fastball soon became as much a liability as it had been an asset. Why?

The primary reason was that Rick Sutcliffe was not the same pitcher any longer. His injuries had changed his physical tools. Rick could no longer be the fastball pitcher of 1984, but not facing the change immediately, Rick spent the next two years allowing his game to slip away. The injuries to his arm seemed to have created a blockade to his future success.

But in 1987, Rick Sutcliffe regained control. Being the intelligent performer he is, Rick finally realized that he had to do something other than depend upon his fastball to succeed. Rather than give up the game, he changed his method. Instead of beating his head against a blockade to success and dooming himself to long-term failure, he went around the obstacle which was preventing him from reaching the level of performance he knew he was capable of.

In 1987, Rick Sutcliffe was no longer a fastball pitcher who only used the breaking ball to set up his fastball. He had changed. Rick Sutcliffe became a curveball pitcher who threw some fastballs to set up his breaking pitches. He evaluated the tools he had in 1987 and changed his game. The goal was the same, only the method was different.

Don't get me wrong, Rick Sutcliffe gave 110 percent effort in 1985 and 1986. His intensity was the same as it had been in the past. He worked as hard to come back from his injuries as anyone I have ever seen. The fact was, though, that for him the game had changed. He could work *with* the new set of rules, or spend the rest of his life fighting *against* them. He chose the first option and was so successful that in 1987 he almost won the Cy Young Award again.

Why was Rick Sutcliffe able to reach his goal even after a very real blockade had been placed in his way? We could ask ourselves the same question of anyone

◆

who seems to face insurmountable obstacles and succeeds nonetheless.

The first defense to a negative belief system is a healthy self-image. Most of us have heard of the extremes that prevent a healthy self-image, those put on children by abusive parents, on adults by an environment which tears them down. These situations exist, certainly, but most of us are not such obvious victims. Most of us go through life thinking we are pretty normal, ordinary people. And we are. And as such, we are overrun by doubts which prevent us from breaking out of our shells and moving forward to claim what we can achieve.

Say this. "In every competition there must be a winner, and there is no reason why that winner can't be me." Say it again. Aloud. Keep saying it until you believe it, because it is true.

If you are competing for a job, you have to approach the interview with an inner assuredness that says, "When you hear my qualifications and become aware of my abilities, you will choose me." Plus you have to radiate this confidence to the person who is interviewing you. In any situation, you must believe that you are better prepared than your competition. More than this, you have to believe you deserve to win. This is part of the process of "psyching out" your opponent. But before you "psyche out" your opponent, you must "psyche out" yourself.

Don't mistake this self-assuredness for simply being cocky. Self-assuredness is built on realities. You are qualified, you have the ability. Cockiness derives from being unprepared. Self-assuredness takes your positives and reinforces them with attitude. Cockiness merely attempts to disguise your negatives with attitude. Once you recognize the difference between the two, it is a simple matter to build up that self-assuredness and overcome any obstacles which seem to be blocking your success. It took some time for me to build up my self-assuredness, but once I did, the payoffs began.

While at college, I was being watched by anybody and everybody who could forward my career. The fact that they might have come to the field to watch Thurman Munson overshadowed my ability to realize this. But I had other problems, or at least I thought I did. One was confidence. Another was size.

Any time a scout spoke with my father about signing me, my size became an issue. I am five feet nine and one-quarter inches tall, although I always listed myself on draft forms as five feet ten inches. The scouts felt I was too small and, therefore, not durable enough to play. The pitchers being drafted at that time were six-foot-three or more and I had heard this size issue brought up enough times to believe it. Was my height a real blockade? I certainly was not going to get any taller. And it got to the point that I started to believe that my goal of playing in the major leagues would be stopped by an issue I could not control.

Luckily for me, my father took me in hand. "Once you're drafted, talent wills out. But before that, the things they use to grade talent can be very detrimental to you. You're never going to be a tall pitcher, son," he said to me. "Therefore you must be a better pitcher."

Time has proven he was right, but it was a long, hard stretch from draft to the Cy Young Award in 1980.

In 1967, I was playing Class A amateur baseball in a city league in Cleveland and doing rather well. Thurman had gone to the Cape Cod baseball league, where he had come to the attention of some major league scouts. When he came back, he suggested to me that I get out of Cleveland, having progressed about as far as I was going to there, and play at Chatham for Joe Lewis. It sounded like a good idea to me, and at the time of the June draft the team

♦

27

assembled in Massachusetts was a powerhouse. We had Thurman behind the plate; I was pitching. Also on board were left-hander John Curtis, Rich McKinney, and outfielder Bobby Valentine.

It was a great experience for me and I felt that finally I was getting the chance to show my talent. When the June draft came around, I was ready. The offers came in. McKinney got $35,000 from the Chicago White Sox; Valentine $65,000 from the Los Angeles Dodgers; Curtis negotiated $100,000 from the Boston Red Sox; and Thurman got in the neighborhood of $110,000 as a first round draft choice for the Yankees. Me? I wound up as the Cleveland Indians sixteenth round draft choice. Their first offer started around $15,000 and worked itself down to $8,000 before the talking just died away. (Remember, the year was 1968, and contract money then was a lot lower than contract money now.)

At that point I got mono and hepatitis and left the Cape. If being sick and losing forty pounds weren't heartbreaking enough, watching the four fellows I was supposed to play ball with that summer sign lucrative contracts just about ended my career. Physically I was weakened, mentally I was devastated.

If I were ever to give up my goal of a major league career, this was the point in time I would have done it. My hopes had been built up and then allowed to drop lower than I could have ever believed they would. Everyone else got the breaks, never me. My entire life in baseball had been one struggle after another. Nothing was ever handed to me. Sure, when I was a kid playing ball it was easy to shine, but the older I got the harder it got. Was I offered the scholarships to college? No, they went to the other guys, and they weren't better ballplayers than I was. When the scouts came to college games to look over the players, did they ever come to look at me? No. And what did I get in the draft? A low pick for a hometown boy. I was

◆

working my way into the best case of blaming everyone else for my misfortunes that I have ever seen. And why not? I had spent the whole summer in bed and had nothing else to do but feel sorry for myself. Life was unfair, just look at what happened to me.

Ironically, it was Thurman Munson who finally pulled me out of my self-pitying state. The Yankees had assigned him to the Double A Eastern League, playing out of Binghamton, New York. The Eastern League is a pitcher's dream with that heavy air and those big ballparks. That year Thurman hit .301, which was a pretty big accomplishment in the Eastern League. Thurman always thought he should have hit .400.

Seeing Thurman after that summer was hard for me. Over the years, he had become more than my teammate, he had become my friend. The days of youthful arrogance had passed and Thurman had grown into very much his own man. Thurman knew there was nothing he could not do and this self-confidence emanated from him. My respect for the man, however, was not without a tinge of envy. He had everything I wanted.

Of course, we talked about his experiences in Binghamton. I listened, interested in what had happened, wanting to know what life was like in the big leagues. However, underneath it all, there was a question nagging at me. Something I had to bring out. The more he spoke, the more the question ate at me. Finally, when I couldn't stand it any longer, I asked him. I had to know. "Am I as good as those guys in the big leagues? Do I have the stuff?" After spending the summer on my back convincing myself that my career was over, this was one of the hardest questions I ever had to ask. And I knew that I might get back an answer I didn't want to hear.

Thurman could have shined me on, telling me something like "Sure, Steve, you got it. All you need is

♦

the right break." Or he could have just told me to give it up, I didn't stand a chance. At that point in time, I would have believed him. But Thurman did neither. He looked me straight in the eye. "You need to work on your control. You need consistency. You can throw as hard as anyone. Your breaking pitch is major league quality. You've got a shot at making it to the bigs. Underneath it all, I think you got the stuff."

Thurman's reinforcement stopped my thinking from going any further downward, but it was my father who turned my attitude around. "What you've got to do is get healthy. Nothing can happen before that. Afterwards, forget about Cleveland, they are not the only team out there. You are good enough. What you've got to do is believe it like I do. Put the summer draft behind you. Focus on the winter draft. If you do, you will succeed."

I took my father's advice to heart. Slowly I began to rebuild my body into shape. I started with exercises to enhance my overall fitness, taking special care to watch my diet and personal regimen. After my body was strong enough, I began to rework my pitching skills. Being off-season, there was ample opportunity to work with the Kent State team as they prepared for their upcoming baseball season. My rehabilitation was planned and determined. I wanted back in the game.

What started out as my biggest streak of bad luck, turned around. The mental and physical effects of my illness, not being signed by Cleveland, and months of depression began to fade. I would like to take credit for regaining control of my own life, certainly to pick yourself up of your own accord is the best type of turnaround, but without my father, it probably would not have been possible.

That winter I was drafted by the San Francisco Giants in the fourth round. So this doesn't seem more than it is, the winter draft is not of the same caliber as

◆

the summer draft. For one thing, there are fewer picks, not as many as forty, and the quality of players available for the draft is generally not as high. Some teams do not even participate. As a matter of fact, the player picked number one that year by San Francisco, Thomas "Joe" Frye, never made it out of spring training. However, on the positive side, I was being given the opportunity to pitch.

Deciding to forego my senior year of college was a big decision. On one hand, I wanted to finish school. By this time, I realized college was more than one big major league training ground. But I didn't think that we would have much of a ballclub that season with Thurman gone to the Yankees. We had just barely been a .500 team with Thurman, and we were also losing our shortstop to graduation. Things looked rather dim for the 1969 Kent State team.

My experience with the Cleveland Indians had taught me not to hold out for money. So when my father and I met with Ray Lucas at the Holiday Inn in Kent, I made it known I just wanted to play pro ball.

The San Francisco roster looked promising for a guy like me. They didn't have many young pitchers, relying mostly on a veteran staff. Juan Marichal, Gaylord Perry, and Ron Herbel were there at the time. The way I saw it, in a few years, I had a good shot at making the major leagues. They offered $10,000 and an incentive bonus of $7,500 when I moved through the minor league system. Finally, this was my chance. I took it.

In 1969, the minor leagues of the San Francisco Giants were stocked with an assortment of hopeful, young players—bright-eyed and waiting for something to happen. There were thirteen new pitchers that first camp in Casa Grande, Arizona, plus another twenty or so who had been sent down through Class AAA and Class AA. Out of these thirty odd pitchers, only two made it to the Class A Fresno team. This

◆

should give you some idea of the odds a player is up against to even make it from a professional camp to one of the minor league teams.

This was my first time away from home for any length of time. As a child, there had not been much money available for vacations so I was not used to travelling and my stint at Cape Cod had been cut short by illness. Talk about someone who had rookie written all over him. I was as excited and anticipatory as every other new player. On the positive side, my arm was in great shape. I was throwing harder and faster than I ever had, about ninety-five miles an hour.

Not that I was the only one in camp with a strong arm. The camp was full of a lot of guys with the same basic talent who were hungry. Some were hungry to begin their careers, while others were hungry to hang on to whatever was left of their careers. I'm sure the rookies, including myself, looked like they had stars in their eyes. Of course, they would—the camp in Casa Grande was the first step toward a dream. Every player there shared the same dream, a ticket to the major leagues. With everyone fighting for the same dream, and the mixture of new players on their way up, and older players who had come down, the competition was fierce.

At the time, I was unaware of how complex the nature of competition was at this camp. Being young and somewhat naive, I went in thinking that talent wills out. And to some extent that was true. If a player did not possess the basic skills to pitch, catch, throw, or hit, he was never going to get past the Fresno camp, that's for sure. But talent wasn't the only thing being tested at this camp. What was also being evaluated was the emotional capacity to play professional sports. Just as many players lost out due to this as did lack of skill.

Many of the rookies either lacked discipline or were unable to focus their discipline properly. I don't mean they didn't show up for practices or behaved inappropriately. This was their big chance, and most were smart enough not to blow it by doing something stupid. The lack of discipline showed more in their control of performance. And the Giant staff watched carefully. For example, could a hitter let the frustration of two bad performances go and take the third at-bat with a relaxed and concentrated attitude? Could a pitcher control the ball time after time even though hitters seemed to be hitting everything he threw at them? Could fielders stay alert? Was a player able to forget what was going on in the rest of his life, and put 100 percent into his effort on the field? Day after day.

The older players who came down were a little different in this respect. They knew the ropes of professional competition. Class A ball did not hold the same mystique. There were those who were jaded, maybe because they knew this was the last stop on the way out. They didn't give it their all. Injuries, age, and disappointment overshadowed any positive attitude they could have had. Most of the older players, though, were just doing their job and doing it to the best of their ability. While we rookies may have had speed and strength, the seasoned players had experience. Sometimes that was worth more than just raw talent. Sometimes not.

My first two roommates in professional baseball were Jerry Pullman, from Utah, and Ed Avila, a Cuban player from Miami. Neither of them made it to the major leagues, Jerry never making it out of Single A and Ed only going as far as Double A, but together we learned about life as professional ballplayers.

Jerry had more desire to play the game of baseball than anyone I had seen up to that point. An ex-football player, he was as tough as nails, as smart as any player I've seen, and as determined as anyone in camp. Unfortunately, he was the victim of one of

◆

life's little tricks—a lack of talent. And the absence of talent finally caught up to him.

Jerry was a shortstop, and the vision of him waiting by second base for a throw was something to behold. He'd stand in there and take all the punishment a runner could deliver. I remember one time when he moved over to cover second base on a sacrifice attempt, but the throw from the catcher tailed into the sliding runner. In those days most of the players used the feet-first slide rather than the head-first slide. And feet first meant spikes first. Well, Jerry dove across the bag like a wide receiver in football to catch the errant throw. His momentum carried him head-on into the sliding base runner's spikes. Trouper that he was, Jerry held on to the ball. He couldn't complete the double play but he did get the force out.

To be honest, as a rookie I took little notice of anyone else's problems or play. I was there to play ball and move up the ranks to the major leagues. I was able to focus on honing my skills and making the most of the talent I knew I had. My highly competitive nature blocked out most of everything else and helped me make the team while others did not.

We had a fairly decent team in 1969. We came very close to winning the first half but got blown out in the second half. At one point, my record was three wins and twelve losses and my ERA was 6.00, hardly major league material, but I was averaging twelve strikeouts per game. Everytime I'd throw a baseball in the wrong spot, somebody would hit a double and I seemed to be destined to be one of those pitchers who would wind up with a losing record, year after year after year. But something happened along the way to change all that. They gave away my uniform in Bakersfield.

I had pitched the night before in Fresno, and the manager said he was going to take my uniform away and give it to a six-foot-five pitcher who was throwing that night. Jesse Huggins, a left-handed pitcher, not only was eight inches taller than me, but he out-weighed me by fifty pounds. Jesse was a sight on the mound. His pants were too short, his sleeves were too short, and he was a little short on his stuff that night because he was yanked early.

I was charting pitches in the stands. It was a very hot night. Bakersfield gets to be 110 to 112 degrees during the summertime and every bug in central California gravitates to the heat. We were at Sam Lynn Field, a field that only had one working shower stall; each and every one of us on the team hoped to get back to the El Rancho Hotel, where we'd at least have the benefit of running water.

It was there in the stands of Bakersfield that I met some people who ultimately changed my life. George and Denise Irvine, great boosters of the Los Angeles Dodgers, lived in Bakersfield and spent their summers watching the Class A Dodgers. I started to talk with them and they turned out to be wonderful people, in fact, our relationship has continued to this day.

I must have appeared to them in need of a real home cooked meal because they invited me back to their home for dinner. "Come to the house," Denise said, "we'll have tacos." Bear in mind, in the 1960s Ohio had not been introduced to Mexican food and I didn't have the slightest idea what a taco was, but I knew that I was destined to have one meal that wasn't ordered off a menu. Whatever it was, I was ready to accept.

I learned about tacos at this dinner, and, now that I make my home in Arizona, tacos are a staple of my diet. But the Irvine's gave me more than an introduction to Southwestern food. During our conversations our mutual admiration of Sandy Koufax came up. They had Sandy's autobiography at the house and they gave it to me to read. Over the next few weeks, read it I did.

♦

Although I couldn't compare Koufax's style or talent to lesser pitchers such as myself, he did say one thing that hit home and went hand-in-hand with the philosophy I developed afterwards. He said the most important pitch in baseball was not a fastball or a curveball or a slider. He said the most important pitch in baseball is strike one. If you can get ahead of the batter by throwing the first pitch for a strike, it puts the batter on the defensive rather than the offensive. Now you only need two more strikes for a strikeout. And if the batter does hit the ball, there are seven men behind you who are on their toes ready to make the play.

Koufax's way of strategizing the game clarified my own method of play. The two ball, no strike, and the three ball, one strike pitches are the most dangerous in baseball. The hitter knows the pitcher has to come to him or risk walking him. The object of pitching then becomes always to stay ahead of the hitter.

That phrase, "The most important pitch in baseball is strike one," turned around my entire season. That and the fact that after reading Koufax's book, I developed a better handle on my own abilities. I could see where his philosophies tied into my own method of play and this built my confidence as a pitcher.

When we played Lodi, the Oakland A's farm team, during the second half of the season in Fresno, I had one of those enchanted nights, one of those games where everything fell into place for me. I struck out seventeen men. In the stands that night was a local product who had made good. Jim Maloney, a star with the Cincinnati Reds, was interviewed after the game by one of the local writers and asked what he thought of the pitcher who had just struck out seventeen men. Maloney said that he felt sure that the young pitcher had major league stuff and predicted that in the very near future that young man would be pitching in the major leagues. Reading the article built my confidence even more.

Forgotten were all of the nightmares of the first half. I had been the starting pitcher in five games where the scores wound up in the twenties against us and was personally responsible for another young pitcher, Rick Hayes, being released from baseball. Hayes and I were the only two pitchers to make it to Fresno from that first camp. But he had the misfortune of being a reliever added to the greater misfortune of always coming into games after I had been ineffective. Once you turn a team on offensively, it is very difficult to turn them off. I would give up five runs in two or three innings and then Denny Sommers, my manager, would take me out and bring in Hayes, who would then just start getting clobbered. Hayes would give up three or four more runs, but Denny, not wanting to waste any more relievers, would leave Hayes in and the slaughter would continue. Mercifully, the game would eventually end, but Hayes wound up with an ERA of around ten. He was released in June.

Even if the team was not doing well, for me the second half had turned around. I later had a fifteen strikeout performance against Modesto. In that game the opposing starting pitcher was a man who later became one of the great relievers in the major leagues, The Mad Hungarian, Al Hrabosky. Al was a master of the psyche-out on the mound, not only psyching out the hitters but psyching up himself. Later in his career he grew an intimidating fu manchu mustache, and had this wild mane of hair. Al would stalk behind the mound, turning his back to the hitter, and put everything together mentally. Then he'd smack the ball into his glove and march onto the mound to deliver his next pitch. The process was not dissimilar from what I developed later on, but The Mad Hungarian did it with flourish.

◆

Another young man from that 1969 season who later turned out to have a successful major league career was George Foster. Unlike Al though, George was a teammate. At the time, George was a very withdrawn young man. He had some talent, but he hadn't really let a lot of it out at that point. The rest of the team thought George a strange man in that here we were in Fresno, a little cooler than Bakersfield at only 104 degrees most every day, and George would sit on the bench when he wasn't playing, with towels wrapped around his waist and neck and a jacket on over the towels. Nobody could figure out what was going on with George, so we just concluded he was a little weird. Nobody realized that this same George Foster, who was creating his own personal steam room, would later get traded from the San Francisco Giants and hit 52 home runs for the Cincinnati Reds in 1977. Before George, the last player to hit 50 or more home runs was Willie Mays, with 52 in 1965. And it wasn't until the 1990 season, when Cecil Fielder of the Detroit Tigers hit 50 home runs, that the barrier was broken again.

In the second half I won nine of my next ten games, finished the season 12–13 with an ERA of 3.60, down from 6.00. Because of this, I was given the opportunity my second year to go to the Double A camp to try and make the Amarillo ballclub.

Without Koufax's book, and learning his view of the mental aspects of pitching, I may not have been able to turn the season around. Koufax's book was not just another I-did-it-this-way volume, because nobody could do it his way. He had a ninety-eight-mile-an-hour fastball and a curveball nobody could hit. The rest of us had to adjust our games any way we could. The philosophy he espoused, though, helped me.

My 1970 year at Amarillo was eventful in that it taught me an amazing thing about talent, what it can do and what it can't do.

♦

The 1969 Amarillo team won the Texas League. The San Francisco Giants organization, at that point, was logjammed with talent. They had a lot of successful hitters and a lot of talented young pitchers at the Triple A level. What that meant was that every one of those players on the winning 1969 team, almost without exception, went back to Amarillo in 1970. These were hungry players in 1969, working their way up the system. They went all out in 1969 to win. The only starting pitcher on the 1970 team who did not play on the 1969 team was me. One would think that in 1970, the same players coming back would have a cakewalk to the championship. The reality was just the opposite occurred. The Amarillo Giants finished last in 1970.

Talent did not win out. In 1970, much of the incentive was taken away from these guys. Good year or not, because of the tremendous talent in the San Francisco organization, there was no place to move up to. Financially, there were not a lot of rewards in the minor leagues in those days. My first year, I made $500 a month. My second year I made $700 a month. A $200 a month raise sounds like a lot, but when you're only playing four and a half months, it really isn't a lot. Maybe in the third year a player could go to $1000 a month. So what the 1969 Amarillo Giants were playing for was a shot at the major leagues. With the realization that even with a good year you wouldn't move up in the organization, the players' attitudes went from determined to lackluster.

The performances were so bad on that 1970 team, that only four of us from that team ever made it to the major leagues. Jim Howarth had a brief stint with the San Francisco Giants, as did pitcher Jim Barr, out of the University of Southern California. The fourth player joined us later in the season, and infused a little life in the team and went on to infuse a great deal of life in the major leagues. The player,

♦

Dave Kingman, also out of USC, went on to become one of the great sluggers in the game.

I was the only pitcher who had a decent year. Bear in mind, I was only in my second year of professional baseball, so I still had a lot of the enthusiasm players have when they still consider themselves on their way up. I did not see the wall up against advancement that some of these guys did, so I worked harder, putting together a solid season for the Giants. I wanted to be ready when my big break came. And the break did come, in the literal sense.

Jim Willoughby, who later made the major leagues, was playing Triple A in Phoenix for the Giants. During an at-bat he squared around to bunt and he took a fastball off his finger and it broke. Being the only pitcher with a winning record in Double A in Amarillo, when it came time for a promotion, the organization gave it to me.

My first game in Triple A was in Eugene, Oregon, against the Philadelphia Phillies team. They had some sluggers on that ballclub, guys who later made it to the Phillies—Willie Montanez, John Vukovich, and Scott Reid, who now is a scout with the Chicago Cubs. I was nervous, needless to say, having my first look at players who had been in the major leagues and now were back down in Triple A, and the cream of the crop of the young players, one step away from the major leagues. The manager of the Giants Triple A team at that time was ex-Cub great, Hank Sauer.

In my first inning of work at Eugene, I loaded the bases with two outs and was facing Scott Reid, a left-handed hitter, with the count at two and two, when Hank Sauer stepped out of the dugout. He took a long time to get to the mound, but he finally did and said "How you doin', *kid?*" "Fine." He nodded, looked around a bit, then said, "Let me tell you somethin', *kid.*" He then glanced towards the hitter and continued, "if you can throw this guy a high, tight fastball,

♦

40

you can strike him out." He looked at me. "Can you throw this guy a high, tight fastball?" I said, "Yeah, I think I can." Hank shook his head and walked away. I stood on the mound and figured if there was any better time to throw a high, tight fastball, I didn't know it. Sure enough, I threw the ball as hard and as fast as I could, which in those days was pretty hard, and it happened to go high and tight. Sauer was right. I struck Scott Reid out. At that point, Hank Sauer became one of my biggest boosters.

The Phoenix team had some of the biggest pitchers I had ever seen in my life. They were enormous. Bob Garibaldi, who later went on to become a basketball referee, was over six-foot-five and weighed 240 pounds. Dick Sparks was about the same height and about 230 pounds. Joe Costello was a bit taller than both of them and weighed over 250. At just a shade over five-foot-nine, and a new player to boot, being surrounded by these behemoths was physically intimidating to say the least. To say they could throw the ball hard would be an understatement. But baseball is a wonderful game, in that it is more forgiving with respect to size than other sports.

Bob Garibaldi had suffered an arm injury just before he signed with professional baseball. Although he had a couple of shots at the major leagues, he was destined not to make it over the long haul.

The other two fellows were an example of what your mind can do for you in allowing you to achieve certain results. On the sidelines, both Joe and Dick threw the ball exceptionally well, probably as well as anybody else in the league. Because they were so big and had a dominating presence on the mound, they had a bit of an advantage. So, watching them on the sidelines, anyone would have thought the two of them would tear the league up. But, much to the dismay of Hank Sauer and the coaches, this was not the case. Whatever these two men had on the sidelines, stayed

♦

there. Neither Joe or Dick was able to cross over that line and take that game to the mound.

Joe and Dick are not alone. There are a lot of players who are excellent in practice but cannot translate that performance into results when the game actually starts. I would say the reason for this lies in these players' self-confidence. They truly don't believe they can do it.

Throwing on the sidelines is easy. You throw the ball as nice and loose as you possibly can. There's no stress. No one's trying to hit the ball back at you. But when you get out into the game, that's when things tighten up, both emotionally and physically. It's a guaranteed thing when throwing a baseball, tighten up mentally and your arm will follow. And when that happens, all the natural movement your ball has will suddenly disappear. That fastball that was hopping up and down, or moving in and out, suddenly goes straight as a string. Believe me, there is no easier pitch for a major league hitter to handle than a straight down the middle fastball.

I was lucky enough that year to play with one of my heros as I was growing up in Ohio—Leon Wagner. Leon broke in with the San Francisco Giants, originally, but he later spent time with the Cleveland Indians, including the 1964 season when he had 31 home runs and 100 RBIs. But Leon Wagner was more than just a teammate that year, he was a mentor of mine. Leon always told me I had the stuff to consistently strike out five or six guys in every major league game.

Leon, along with Jimmy Ray Hart, a former Giants star also playing for Phoenix, gave me reason to pause. They both had played out their careers pretty well, and now, at the end they still came out every day and played the game hard. As a young man, I wondered what the incentive was. I couldn't see much of a future for either one of them. They were never going

♦

to achieve the same success they had earlier in their careers, and what got them out to the ballpark every day was beyond me.

Over time, they both had experienced enough injuries to lessen their level of performance, as all players do. But more than the physical injuries, at twenty-two, I thought the mental effect of not being able to do the things that you once were able to do would be enough to take yourself out of the game. There were pitchers on the mound getting them out on pitches that ten years earlier they would have crushed. The hand speed wasn't there any longer. The eyesight wasn't quite as good.

I would have thought that enough to get them out of the game, but it wasn't. Every day both Leon and Jimmy Ray were out at the ballpark giving it their all, which at times wasn't a whole lot at that point. Although I wasn't in the same position as Leon and Jimmy Ray, being a younger player with no place to go but up, I promised myself that I would never be in the position they were. I would know when it was time to quit. I would know when my skills were gone. With the self-assuredness of youth, I told myself I would always leave this game before they asked me to and never be one just to hang around because there was nothing else in my life.

Later, I did just that; however, maturity added the measure of soul-searching both Leon and Jimmy Ray must have experienced as they made their decisions to carry on or retire.

That first Triple A season I went 5–3, with an ERA of 1.71, standing the Pacific Coast League on their ear. Coming on the heels of a 12–13 year in 1969, I went a combined 14–8 for the 1970 season and established the fact that I could throw the ball on the Triple A level. This got me my invitation to the major league camp in 1971. Without Hank Sauer in my corner, I probably would not have been given the opportunity.

♦

In my first spring training in 1971, I was the second man to throw batting practice. The first man to throw batting practice, as was the tradition in the San Francisco Giants training camp in Casa Grande, Arizona, was Juan Marichal. The first couple of hitters up were the first hitters in the order, Bobby Bonds would hit first followed by Hal Lanier and Tito Fuentes, and then Willie Mays would hit. Everybody would throw five minutes of batting practice. Most of the pitchers weren't ready yet which was fine because most of the hitters weren't ready yet, either. The tradition went, Juan, who had great control, would get up and lay one in, and Willie would hit one out of the park.

There were a lot of reporters around that day, being the first day of spring training. Juan got up and pitched his five minutes, which was all that was allotted. After three hitters, I was given the opportunity to pitch. Unlike most of the other players, though, I had been in training for two months. I didn't look at this as spring training. Because I was a non-roster player, this was my World Series. I knew that if I didn't pop some eyes during spring training, I would be lost in the shuffle.

At that time, I threw the ball over ninety miles an hour. I was the hardest throwing pitcher in the San Francisco Giants organization, which was why, even as a non-roster player, I was given the opportunity to come and pitch at the Giants camp. Also, it was the practice to bring a lot of young pitchers in for batting practice to save the arms of the veteran staff.

But I had a game plan going in. Starting January 1, I threw batting practice to a catcher from a high school team in Scottsdale, Arizona. By the time spring training rolled around, I was throwing as well and as hard as I ever had.

As I warmed up, the smell of the new mown grass and the capsulin, which is an analgesic, on my arm triggered my senses. I was as pumped up as I had ever been. This was my first time on the mound against major league hitters. I looked up, and the first hitter into the cage was Willie Mays, number 24, the future Hall-of-Famer, the outfielder against whom, not only his generation, but every other generation of outfielder is measured. So there I was, against tradition, firing bullets on the opening day of camp.

Willie was popping everything up and could barely hit the ball out of the cage. Willie turned to Dick Dietz, who had been the All-Star catcher in 1970 when he hit .300. "Who is that kid out there?"

Dietz shrugged. "Just some young kid trying to make an impression."

"Well, tell him it ain't the World Series. Go out there and tell him to get the ball over the plate."

Dick stood up, put his catcher's mask over his head, and walked out to the mound. By this time all of the reporters were focusing in on Dick and I. Dick says, "Look kid, it's a tradition around here. Juan lays them in, Willie hits them out of the park and all the reporters write that Willie Mays gets up out of bed and hits home runs. So just lay them in to Mays, and you can throw hard to the next guy."

The sweat was pouring down my face and my adrenalin was pumping. I said to Dick Dietz, "You tell Willie to go screw himself. If he doesn't like it, tell him to get out of the cage."

Dick just looked at me to see if I was serious. I guess he decided I was because he put his mask back on and went back to the plate. He told Willie, "I don't think he's going to take it easy."

The next pitch, I threw as hard as I could and Mays hit it straight up into the cage. He took his bat and fired it straight into the side of the batting cage, never to take batting practice off me again in my two-year tenure with the San Francisco Giants.

At dinner that night, some of the players, mostly the younger ones, came up to me. "Hear you and

Willie had an argument today." "No," I said, "not an argument. Just a difference in philosophy. Willie knows he's going to make the team. I don't know if I am, so I've got to throw hard every time out."

While that day at batting practice, I had all the confidence I needed, overall that spring training of 1971 was a time of great insecurity. Every pitcher at that camp went through a check list daily, knowing that the hard reality was that only ten of us would break camp with the San Francisco team. Figuring the players who already had major league experience were almost guaranteed to make the team, you realized that, depending upon trades and injuries, there were at most two spots available. With between twenty to twenty-two pitchers in camp, the odds did not look good—for anyone.

Fighting for the final two spots were Jim Willoughby, Skip Pitlock, Frank Reberger, Don Carrithers, and me. From among this group, my most direct competition was Skip Pitlock.

Skip was a left-handed pitcher out of Southern Illinois University. He joined us in Fresno in the middle of the 1969 season. Coming out of a college in mid-year, he got his opportunity to pitch, and did pretty well. We were two of the shining stars in the lower minor league level for the San Francisco Giants. As it turned out, we were both invited to try out for Double A ball in Amarillo that next year.

Although we were in competition with each other as starting pitchers, Skip had a decided advantage being a lefty. With right-handed pitchers dominating the Amarillo roster, a left-handed pitcher had the advantage, assuming the talent was the same, because there were fewer of them. This was frustrating for me because I felt he was given more opportunities simply because he was a left-hander.

However, at the same time we were invited to Amarillo, the Giants Triple A team needed a left-handed pitcher. The Triple A manager at the time was Charlie Fox, who later moved up to manage the Giants. Skip did pretty well in the Triple A training camp for the short time he was there. As it turned out, in mid-1970, the Giants themselves needed a left-handed pitcher, and, since Skip had done well for the organization so far, he was moved up to the major leagues. So, after starting out in the same place in 1969, Skip had made it to the majors by the middle of the 1970 season while I was only in Triple A.

The way I had it figured in 1971, there was one spot open in the starting rotation and possibly one in the bullpen. That left Skip and I going head to head, once again.

My psychological approach that first spring training really paid dividends in my battle against Skip. Skip already viewed himself as a major league pitcher, having gone 5–5 in his first season with the Giants. I was a non-roster player coming to spring training, and every performance for me was life or death with respect to my future in the game. And I had been throwing for two months. Skip, on the other hand, viewing the open spot as his, signed, sealed, and delivered, used spring training as many major league players do, as a time to round into shape.

On the surface, Pitlock's philosophy wasn't a bad one. Here is a time when the stats don't count, the wins and losses don't count, the early performance doesn't count. Veteran players use this time to rehone their skills so by the time the regular season rolls around they are ready. For veteran players, it's the correct attitude. Once I had reached the point where my position on the team was assured, I used spring training to round into shape. But only when I was assured a spot.

That's where Skip made his mistake. He assumed that since he had a fairly good season the year before with the Giants, he could take advantage of this time

♦

to rehone his skills. The problem was that Skip did not have a long enough history to base his assumption on. Where Skip might have looked upon himself as a veteran major leaguer, the organization viewed him as an up-and-comer with still a lot to prove. Where Skip might not have been 100 percent that first day of spring training, my determination and preparation assured that I was. I was the one who was hungry. I was the one with a game plan. I was the one who was ready to bring every bit of competitive energy to bear. I was the one who was focused.

Willie Mays was right. I did look at every time on that mound as my World Series. Every time out I made sure I was at the peak of my game. As I saw it, I had everything to gain and nothing to lose. My only guarantee when I entered the camp was that I'd be throwing batting practice to major league hitters. Skip assumed he had a guaranteed job. As the camp went on, though, it became more and more obvious who had the guarantee and who did not.

When the starting rotation was announced for the 1971 season, Juan Marichal was the number one pitcher, Gaylord Perry number two, and I was number three.

Skip Pitlock went on to spend some time in the major leagues, including parts of two seasons with the Chicago White Sox, but he never got out of his career what he thought he should. Even though he had the advantage of being a left-handed pitcher and had some talent, he never had what would be considered a great career. I believe the reason why I succeeded at that first camp and in future years where Skip did not was my emotional outlook. I did not assume that anything was guaranteed. I had a clear understanding of where I stood and what I had to do to keep my career moving forward.

I could have easily let either one of the obstacles I ran up against in 1968, my illness or my experience

♦

with the Cleveland Indians, prevent me from pushing on toward my goal. Without the help and support of men like my father and Thurman Munson, I might have. My negative belief system was such that I seemed to need someone else to give me that shove forward. I was lucky, that time. But how many of us are faced with what may seem like insurmountable obstacles and have no one to steer us back to the right track? What happens if they're not there? We cannot depend on those around us to turn us around. We need to be able to reach deep within ourselves for that strength. At any time, we have to have the power to motivate ourselves toward our goal. A healthy self-image is the basis for that power.

Don't get the idea that once I signed with a major league team these self-imposed blockades, my doubts or my reliance on the strength of others, went away. Far from it. The negatives about my size, my endurance, my power, and my strength were simply replaced by . . . the New York Yankees. During my career, playing against the Yankees was like showing up to lose.

Before every game I ever pitched against the New York Yankees, I'd be in the bullpen telling myself, "Jeez, I have bad stuff today." "My arm hurts." "My timing's off." "I always have bad stuff against the Yankees." Consequently, whenever I'd go out against the Yankees, I never seemed to be at the top of my game and they would always beat me. In 1973, when Thurman Munson was still a member of the Yankees, I lost to them twice in the same week, 2–1 and 2–0. Somedays I had some pretty good stuff against the Yankees, but I could never seem to make that big pitch when I needed to. Something always happened. Guaranteed. I never did beat the Yankees in 1973. Nor did I in 1977, 1978, or 1979. Before every game, I'd think to myself, "I hope I don't have the same bad stuff that I had in my last game against the Yankees." I wasn't surprised, though, when I did.

♦

Talk about a negative self-image. I may not have realized the Yankees had me, but they sure did. The Yankees didn't have to psyche me out, I did that on my own. I pitched poorly. Meanwhile, I just thought I needed some good stuff. What I really needed was some positives in my behavior, a little self-confidence, belief in myself, a better self-image.

One of the best places to start building self-image is to bring yourself back to a time when your performance was at its peak. Maybe it was some sports competition where you gave that extra 10 percent. It could have been at work the day you spent that little extra time to do an exceptional job. The Saturday afternoon you spent teaching your child how to ride a bike. Everyone of us has a moment we can call our best. Go back to that moment. It doesn't matter what you were doing, what matters is the attitude with which you approached the task. You probably looked forward to it, anticipated it, thought about it over and over before actually doing it. Remember the feeling?

Now think of another moment when you performed well. When you examine it, I'm sure you will find similarities with the first incident you thought of. The positive attitude. The excitement. The pride. Now think of another. Take a moment and keep bringing up these times in your past when success came naturally. See yourself perform. Let yourself go. If the moment was physical remember how you moved. Feel your body move now. If your muscles tense, that's okay. If the moment you brought to mind was mental, reapproach the task. Let your mind go back to the thoughts which preceded your performance. Experience the anticipation. Go through it. Smile when it's over.

If you've actually done what I asked you to do, you've begun to develop the basic technique of creative visualization. There's nothing magical about it. Creative visualization is making the mind see your performance as if you were outside yourself looking

◆
50

in. And I bet just thinking of these positive moments brought back the same thrill of achievement.

Wouldn't it be great if we could feel this way all the time, about everything we do?

Part of the reason Earl Weaver was not able to convince me that I had failed as a pitcher was the memory of that day in Casa Grande when I threw against Willie Mays. Sure, there had been many winning games in which I had simply done well enough to get by, but I knew what I was capable of achieving. If I could pitch as well as I did that one day at batting practice, then I was able to pitch that well again. The challenge was to bring myself to a level to repeat the success.

I used this memory to rebuild my confidence. Like Rick Sutcliffe in 1987, I was faced with meeting my goal with a different set of tools. Over the years, injuries had taken their toll. More than ten years had passed since that Giants batting practice, and I was not as strong or quick as I had been in my younger days, but none of that mattered. I knew I was capable of superior performance.

My mind dwelled on this practice. I let myself relive the strength and power I felt that day. I even found myself throwing mythical pitches as I walked around my apartment. The more I thought about that day in Casa Grande, the more sure of myself I became. I could feel the strength coming back to my arm, the quickness returning to my movements. I literally convinced myself that I was that pitcher of time passed. And once I started, it became easier.

We all want to be at our peak all the time, but not all of us want to pay the price of getting there. It is a mistake to think that the effort to improve and succeed is harder the more you try. The truth is, it is easier. Once we get into a pattern of positive thought, it becomes our natural state.

We've all heard the example of a glass half-full or half-empty. Take this a step further. When you are

◆

asked to do something you've never done before, do you first think of reasons why you can't? If you do, you probably never break out of your daily pattern. Like Fred at the office who hates Mondays, you look upon life in negative terms. While you might not consider yourself an unhappy person, enthusiasm and excitement are certainly missing. And you have to get these qualities back.

Training yourself to look at the positives, the ways you *can*, is the first step in achieving success and an integral part of a healthy self-image. Talk to yourself. Pump yourself up. Take yourself out of negative situations. Find the positives. Sound almost like self-hypnosis? Well, it is. And it is one of the most powerful tools in the world.

The idea that we are all failures if we want to be is true. But it is a bit extreme for most of us. We don't sit around consciously deciding to fail and we don't gripe and complain about everything that occurs in our lives. If we did, we would be quite alone. No, for most of us, the negative attitudes are more subtle and we have to work at identifying them. In order to do this, we have to honestly evaluate ourselves.

Remember, we are our own worst critics.

What are your positives? Make a list. Put them all down. If you know you're intelligent, write it down. Are you a good athlete? Generous? A gifted musician? Can you sing? Is your spaghetti sauce the best you've ever tasted? Do you have a sense of humor? Take as long as you like to make this list and forget nothing.

If you've been honest with yourself, you've probably filled a page or two. Now look at the list. With all these great qualities, you're dealing with a pretty terrific person. If you knew someone who was as good as the person on your list, you sure wouldn't let him keep knocking himself down. As his friend, you'd build him up, wouldn't you? That's exactly what you've got to do for yourself.

♦

You don't dwell on your friends' negatives, so don't dwell on your own. Concentrate and build on the positives. Each time you find yourself drawn to the down side of a situation, force yourself to recall something that would turn the situation around to a positive. Rick Sutcliffe may have lost something off his fastball, but he had the stuff to build on his curveball. Look at everything in your life with the same attitude. In time you will find there are no blockades to success, only obstacles which can be overcome.

Your attitude toward winning will change from "why me?" to "why not me?" And, why not you?

Successful Meditation

Have you ever been plagued by a tune playing over and over in your head and been unable to think of its title? Or how about your high school math teacher, the one who thought algebra was fun? Have you ever spent hours trying to remember her name? Once I spent an entire day trying to think of the name of the actor who played Sidney Greenstreet's sidekick in *The Maltese Falcon*. I could see him, bug eyes and all, hear his weasely voice, even see him holding his cigarette in the underhanded way foreign movie villains do, but I couldn't think of his name.

I tried not to think about it, hoping the answer would suddenly pop into my head. All day I consciously avoided asking myself the question. I ran through the alphabet hoping to trigger some recognition. Remembering this man's name became more important than whatever I needed to remember it for.

Trivial points of fact, I know, but this mental blockage is indicative of what happens to all of us when we let our minds become cluttered. Millions of bits of information enter our brains each day and become encoded in our memories. Most of these facts are useless, like what our spouses wore to work or the telephone number of a pesty salesman. What can be worse than having some jingle haunt you hour after hour and not be able to shake it? Sometimes this bombardment of data crowds relevant thoughts from our conscious minds.

What we need is a way to rest our conscious mind during the day, sort of a mental nap, to sort through the clutter and reevaluate the day's events with respect to what is important, where we are, where we are going, and where we really want to be. We need to take a look at our actions, not just reactions, and decide whether or not we are progressing toward the goals we have set for ourselves. We need to separate the wheat from the chaff.

It would be easy if we could sit down and demand our minds to erase all the useless information, the negative input, the counterproductive thoughts that have accumulated in our heads. Poof, they'd be gone and we'd be sitting there with a ready slate which would only accept positive essential thoughts that help us toward our goals. If this were possible, we'd all be just where we wanted to be. Unfortunately, it's not that easy. Like everything that is worthwhile, a success oriented mind-set takes work and not everyone is willing to put forth the effort.

My first goal after the confrontation with Earl Weaver at the All-Star break was to win the game against the Oakland A's. While many other things

◆

entered my mind during this time, I realized that the only relevant item on my personal agenda was that game. I had to find a way to remove all other thoughts and concentrate on the task at hand. I realized that whenever I felt overwhelmed by a problem and slept on it, I usually awoke with the answer. A common occurrence, and with good reason.

While we sleep, our conscious minds relax, the barriers we have built to protect ourselves from outside forces break down and our subconscious minds take over. In our sleep, we can see ourselves as the boss, naturally beautiful, a scratch golfer. In our dreams, anything is possible.

Just as my confrontation with Earl consumed my thoughts during the day, my dreams were filled with images of my career—past, present, and future. I would awake with bits and pieces of insight—how I could overcome the problem of a weak arm, a strategy for dealing with Earl more effectively, a game plan against this batter or that one. Each morning I would have another fragment, but this series of piecemeal realizations was not enough. I needed to harness the mental energy that was in my subconscious, focus it on the game against Oakland, and remember every thought. All this without spending the entire day asleep.

The process of "sleeping on it" came close to my recollections of what I had read about meditation. I recalled that the process involved relaxed, concentrated thought; however, I couldn't focus in on a particular meditation theory that pertained to my need. What I did remember, though, was that visualizing yourself in a given situation, seeing yourself perform as you wanted to perform, doing the thing that you desired to do, was the foundation for improving performance. I put the two theories, meditation and creative visualization, together.

Ten days after the All-Star break, two hours before the most important game of my entire career, I laid down on my bed, relaxed, closed my eyes, and focused every bit of mental energy I could muster. Then I pitched the game.

I visualized the stadium, heard the noise of the crowd, let the tension build. I watched myself move toward the mound. I saw the lineup. Rickey Henderson was the first Oakland hitter. His face came to me as he walked to the plate. I scrutinized his stance, studied his movement. I thought of the pitch, how it should feel, where I wanted the ball to go. I saw Rickey settle in at the plate. I wound up and threw. Strike one.

I heard the crowd shout their approval as the catcher threw the ball back to me. I stepped off the mound and took a deep breath. My arm felt great. I got back in position. The batter positioned himself. I wound up. I felt myself pitch. The ball flew past the bat and I heard it slam into the catcher's glove. Strike two.

The crowd got louder. I felt the sun. I thought of nothing but that next pitch. I concentrated on the feel of the seams, how I took my arm back, how my weight shifted when I finally released the ball from my hand. I threw. The batter swung and as the ball embedded itself in the catcher's glove, the crowd went wild. Strike three.

The rest of the game followed suit. Each batter in succession struck out. Every pitch was executed perfectly. My arm felt good and the crowd stayed with me. My mind conjured the rhythm, that precise physical groove that allowed me to handle the ball with pinpoint accuracy. As the game progressed, I felt myself grow stronger. My mind, my body, the crowd, and the game merged into one.

Needless to say, I pitched a perfect game, twenty-seven outs. And why not? These were my thoughts and I was conditioning myself to be the best I could be. If I couldn't conceive of myself as a winner, I knew I'd never be one.

♦

I envisioned the newpaper the next day. Headlines read "Stone Pitches Perfect Game." Baltimore fans sung my praises. "Best pitcher on the team." "Smartest free agent choice in years." My record changed before my eyes, 7–7. Earl slapped me on the back, "Great game." Even my picture in the newspaper made me better looking. When life is on an upswing, why limit it?

After I had finished playing the game in my mind, I went to play the game on the field. Consciously I maintained the attitude I had built that afternoon. And that positive feeling stayed with me. I reviewed my game plan and stuck to it. As I pitched that day, there were no thoughts of lucky hits, bad hops or "due for a bad one." I had no doubt that I was a winner. That day I beat Oakland—ten strike-outs, no walks, a complete game. The final score was 4–1.

Some would call my mental preparation daydreaming, but, in reality, it was meditation. No, there were no gurus or sitars, only myself and my subconscious. Because that's all meditation is, the conscious mind getting in touch with the subconscious. And we all do it one way or another whether we realize it or not.

Think back to those few moments before sleep, while you lie in bed, relaxed. Remember how the day's issues become clearer and the solutions to problems more defined. What about on the sofa on a Saturday afternoon, that half-sleep state that comes over you as you shut off the rest of the world and let your mind wander? It may be unfocused; and it may not have purpose; you may not realize you're doing it; but it's meditation.

Meditation is "in" now for anyone interested in quitting smoking to losing weight to just about anything else. Now I'm asking you to look at it as a tool for success. And just as there is nothing mystical about the process, there is nothing "hip" about it either.

♦

Meditation, in some form or other, has existed ever since the first man sat down to examine his thoughts, his feelings or his goals. We just didn't have a label for it. Now that you do, you can learn how to use it.

Suppose you have set up a meeting with your boss next week to cover some things going on at work. Not good things, of course, because who sits down with the boss to discuss what's right? You're nervous about the meeting. The things you have to say have to be said just right. Your boss has a reputation for flying off the handle and you don't want to be his next target. You want the discussion to go smoothly *and* the boss to see your point. You think about the meeting constantly. But is this mental energy constructive? If it's not, make it so.

Find a quiet place, somewhere comfortable, where you can be undisturbed. I usually lay down in bed, but, for you, a hammock in the back yard may be just the spot. Now, relax. I realize that for some people that's easier said than done, but with concentration, you can make your body let go of the stress that tightens both your muscles and your thoughts.

First, relax your feet. Then relax your calves. Work up to your thighs. Tell yourself to do it. Picture the stress passing out of your body. Then move to your arms. When you have relaxed from your hands to your shoulders, relax your back. Concentrate on each step. Your neck, then your face.

It takes a bit to do at first, but this exercise accomplishes two things. First, it puts you in the proper frame of mind to begin your meditation. Second, it builds your ability to concentrate. If this process is particularly difficult for you, don't make an obstacle out of the method. Go to any bookstore and buy a tape made for relaxation. There are dozens.

When your body is relaxed and your mind is clear, bring your thoughts to the meeting with your boss.

♦

Fill in what you will say. Practice the words. See yourself speak. Visualize how your boss will respond. Use what you know of his attitudes and past behavior to anticipate every possible reaction to what you have to say. Vary how you present your arguments. Test the response. What you originally planned to say may need to be changed. You see yourself making relevant, intelligent arguments in a calm, clear manner. To be even more prepared, concentrate on diffusing any emotional and counterproductive points the boss might interject with reasonable and accurate statements. There is no need to feel embarrassed, your thoughts are completely private. You should not only visualize what you will say, see yourself move. How will you sit? Will you stand instead? Do not underestimate the power of body language.

You see yourself leaving the meeting, having accomplished your goal. You feel energized. For good measure, envision your boss informing his boss of what an invaluable employee you are. If your thought process has been productive, what you have done is prepare yourself for a successful meeting.

Sounds simple enough, but if it were, everybody would be doing it all the time. Actually, the process is as simple and natural as it seems, the difficulty most people have in using it is the discipline required to tune ourselves in to it. Meditation takes time, it takes concentration, and it takes the willingness to let go of the barriers we use to protect ourselves from the world around us.

Once is not enough. To be truly effective, this method must become part of your daily life. You must commit to facing the negatives that exist in your subconscious, wiping them away and replacing them with positives. You must set a time each day for meditation and stick to it. You must let your mind be free to think anything it wants, no restrictions. If you limit your thoughts, you limit your goals.

♦

Be aware that unproductive thoughts will just as easily insure you don't reach your goals as productive ones insure you will. If for the week in advance, you only think of how nervous you are and how your boss is going to put down everything you say, you can guarantee yourself that your presentation will bring about those results. You are what you think.

Our minds are powerful instruments and should be kept well-tuned and just a bit pampered. In order to develop meditation into an efficient tool for success, time should be set aside during each day to allow our minds to rest, discover ourselves, and plan our next step toward our goals, whether there is an immediate problem or not. There is nothing wrong with meditating for the sheer pleasure of it.

When I was still playing baseball, I found that meditating for two hours before each game was the most beneficial technique. As a matter of fact, my daily pattern before each game became a ritual. In Baltimore, I would get up around eight in the morning, read the paper, and rummage around the house. Then around ten, I'd go out for something to eat. I had a favorite restaurant not too far from my home where the food was good and the atmosphere relaxed. At that time of the morning, the place wasn't too crowded, so I was able to enjoy some friendly conversation to boot. After breakfast, I would take a short walk, maybe browse through a bookstore or just enjoy the scenery, then return home by noon for a little reading. At two, I'd lay down and visualize the game.

The system worked. In a period of eighteen months, I took myself from a sub-five hundred pitcher to a Cy Young Award winner. During this period, I went from a lifetime 73–79 record to being undefeated in my next thirteen starts and closed the 1980 season with a record of 25–7.

The second game after my turnaround came against the Chicago White Sox. I went head-to-head

♦

against Rich "Tex" Wortham, out of the University of Texas. I was throwing the ball exceptionally well, but so was Tex. I ended up with a no decision, leaving in the eighth with the score tied one to one. The game eventually went into extra innings.

To give you an idea of the kind of specialist Earl Weaver was, he had us work on a play in spring training that could only be used in one eventuality. The play was only to be used with us facing a left-handed pitcher in the late innings of a game when it could win us the game. The pitcher preferably had to be young as far as experience was concerned. The situation was supposed to present itself like this. Runners on first and third, with a fairly weak hitter up. The left-hander would have his back to the man at third base, looking at the man at first base. We worked on this play in spring training for this eventuality, knowing it might only occur once in a year, or once every two years.

All the conditions were right in this White Sox game. The young man on the mound in the tenth inning of this game was Guy Hoffman. He was a rookie. Earl had waited patiently for a half season for his opportunity to use this play. Eddie Murray was on third and Gary Roenicke was on first. The bottom of the order was up.

The man at first was to take a couple of steps off with the pitcher in his stretch. The pitcher, because he was a young man, ideally would have all of his concentration on the man at first, waiting for a quick break to second base. As soon as the man at first would make his break, if the timing was right, the guy at third would break for the plate. Because the pitcher would have to take a couple of steps off the mound to throw to first, the idea was he would never be able to right himself to throw home. Earl had his plan and it was executed perfectly. Being a rookie pitcher, Hoffman was a little excited late in the ballgame. And

♦

when Roenicke took a couple of steps off first, and Murray broke for the plate, Hoffman behaved as Earl expected. Murray scored and we had an extra-inning victory.

The second half of the 1979 season I had thirteen starts, won five and got a no decision in eight.

After all of Earl's threats to go to three pitchers at the end of the 1979 season, conditions changed. Earl never did go to three pitchers. He didn't have to because the team was sailing right along, easy time to the division championship. For all practical purposes, we had it won by the time September came around. All five of our starters were throwing so extremely well, Earl wanted to keep everybody strong for the post season. As a result, I got to pitch on a regular basis the second half of that year and threw the ball very well. True to his word, since I was throwing the ball well, Earl continued to start me.

We faced the California Angels in the American League Championship Playoffs. The Angels were led by MVP Don Baylor, while we had Mike Flanagan, owner of a 23–9 record and the Cy Young Award winner. Our pitching staff held Baylor to just three hits in sixteen at-bats (.186), and the entire Angels team batted just .234. We took the series three games to one, with Scott McGregor posting a complete game shutout victory in the championship game. In all we used only five pitchers in the series—none of which were me.

The heartbreak of the season came in the World Series against the Pittsburgh Pirates. Up three games to one and knowing the final two games were in our park, we were confident that we could win one more game and with it the World Series. But Willie Stargell and company had other ideas. To Pittsburgh's theme song that year, "We Are Family," the Pirates came back from a two-game deficit to win the Series in seven games.

♦

The Pittsburgh win was a classic example of a whole team using a rallying point, focusing energy and concentration, and turning around a performance for a win when every indication would have pointed to a loss.

There is no doubt in my mind that the Baltimore Orioles were a better team. Man for man, position for position, the skill and talent of the Orioles far exceeded anything Pittsburgh could offer. For the first four games of the series, this superiority won out, and it looked as if we were going to close the series after just five games. But tragedy struck, first to the Pirates, and then to the Orioles.

Chuck Tanner was the manager of the Pirates that year, and during the World Series Chuck's mother passed away. Being a member of a team means more than simply working together toward a specific goal. Social dynamics take hold and what happens to one member of the team affects every other member. When Chuck's mother died, the whole team suffered and out of this tragedy came a renewed commitment. It seemed as if the whole team just rallied together. They wanted to do something for Chuck to help him through his grief. And they did.

Suddenly this team which looked all but defeated found a renewed spirit. Even knowing they had to come back to Baltimore for the final two games, didn't daunt them. They were family and all of these players began to play as one. When I think about what that team went through at that point in time, I am still amazed.

I realize two hours of meditation a day is out of the question for most people, and I am in no way advocating that. Just ten minutes quiet time in a quiet place. How about those few minutes you showed up early to the movie theater? Relax with your own thoughts. Or at the breakfast table in the morning.

♦

Wouldn't a quick visualization of the day be more helpful than reading the paper? With enough practice, you can even meditate on the bus in the morning if you don't drive to work. Wherever you choose to meditate, the only criteria is that you are comfortable and you can take your mind away from your surroundings and concentrate on reaching inside yourself to your deepest thoughts.

A couple of years later, when faced with another situation which required my most concentrated effort, the system proved itself again. After my retirement in 1982, ABC approached me with handling the color commentary on "Monday Night Baseball." I had done a limited amount of television, the standard telethons and commercials most athletes do, but not the scope required for nationally televised sports. Since broadcasting was where I determined my future lie, I needed to perform well. Only this time I didn't have two weeks to prepare, I had two days.

Using the same basic techniques, I visualized myself in the broadcast booth, making relevant comments about the game. I heard myself being clever and knowledgeable and saw myself as the viewers would. I felt myself calm and collected. I even heard Al Michaels compliment me on my performance. On the day of the broadcast, I was ready. I was witty and relevant, and, without being told, I knew I had done a great job. Therefore, it was no surprise when Al Michaels really did compliment me after the game. "I've never seen a newcomer do as well. You're going to be all right."

No, meditation does not forsee the future. But, when you do a good job, it's natural to be complimented on it. I saw a successful performance, and recognition is a normal result of success. As a matter of fact, meditation can be so powerful, sometimes it is difficult to tell the difference between experiencing your success mentally and actually living it.

◆

As I became more adept at my meditations before the games, the quicker and deeper I went into the meditative state. More and more details pertaining to the game would fill my mind, so the sensation of the experience became more real.

Once, in Baltimore, I lay down as I usually did, and directed myself to the Seattle Mariners game that evening. As usual, I began by visualizing the stadium and the fans, let myself see the lineup, positioned myself on the mound. But something happened during this meditation that had never happened before. The intensity of concentration was so great that when I awoke I was sure the game was already over. I rubbed my shoulder; it felt great, no pain. It took me a moment before I realized that the game hadn't even begun.

I hadn't spent any longer on this meditation than any of the others, but my mind was so conditioned to accept the positive, relevant input that I was able to concentrate on my performance on a level that I had never experienced before. I was exhilarated. I was going to win that day, all I had to do was get to the field and do it.

I accomplished two things during the Mariners game. I pitched my first, and coincidentally, my only, complete game shutout while in a Baltimore Oriole uniform. The second, and some would say more important thing for the social life of my teammates, I completed the game in less than two hours. I meditated. I visualized. I performed.

This free flow of information between the conscious and subconscious mind is part of the reason we can go to sleep with questions and wake up with answers. The sleep cycle naturally eliminates the conscious mind's control over thought and allows the subconscious mind to take over. Unlike the meditation process, thoughts during the sleep process are uncontrolled. However, if the conscious mind is pre-

♦

occupied with a subject during the day, it has an effect on the subconscious. Our subconscious dreams are triggered by our conscious thoughts and have a lasting effect on our attitudes and behavior.

So don't be surprised if you wake up one morning like I did and your first thought of the day is "Peter Lorre."

5

Erase the Negative Belief System

In baseball, there is a vast wasteland of major league pitchers called middle relief. No one has a good middle relief staff. This is because it is the *one* position in all of baseball that is built on failure. It encompasses all the failed stoppers. (It is an art to get the twenty-fifth, twenty-sixth, and twenty-seventh outs of a game. The stopper has become baseball's golden boy.) And all the failed starters. (A starter must have enough stuff to face each hitter at least three times and still get him out. Completing 25 percent of his starts is also a big plus.) All these pitchers who failed at either end of the spectrum are lumped together in this void called middle relief. And I was right in there with them for about half of my career.

♦

One of the things I realize as I look back is that those years when I was given the ball, I was successful. In 1975 with the Cubs, who were not a particularly good ballclub at the time, I went 12–8 and among starters was tied for the team lead in winning percentage. I got the ball in 1977 all year long with the White Sox. I won fifteen and led the staff in victories. Again I got the ball in 1978 and won twelve, which wasn't a great deal, but I did lead the staff in victories. And I got the ball during all of 1980, won twenty-five and won the Cy Young Award. The four years in my career I was given the ball all year long as a starter, I was a successful pitcher, and those years I was shuffled in out of the bullpen were tough ones.

What did I do those four years that I didn't do in the others? I certainly wasn't a different pitcher. These years were in the second half of my career, not the first half, so I can't claim age or greater physical strength. It wasn't the team. I had played with the Cubs from 1974 through 1976. The White Sox were not an outstanding team in 1977 or 1978. And 1979, my first year with the Orioles, started out dismally. What was the key to those successful years?

I know now. Those years when I was given the ball as a starting pitcher in the rotation, I had greater confidence in myself, a higher belief in my own self-worth. In those years when I came out of the bullpen, my own level of self-esteem was decided by someone else's view of my value to the team. If someone else thought I was essential to the team's success, I was. If not, I faded back into the wasteland. It was almost as if I had traded my father's and Thurman's influence in the early years of my career for my current manager's input.

My years with the Cubs, although not great years, were decent years. My cumulative record over those three years was 23–20; in 1974, I went 8–6, 1975, I went 12–8, and in 1976, a year during which I suffered arm problems, I went 3–6. I was better than a .500 pitcher for a team that was substantially under .500 those three years.

We had some great characters with the Chicago Cubs in those days. Jose Cardenal, still loved by Cub fans today, set the record for the most incredible excuse for missing a fly ball. Jose claimed he lost it in a 747 flying out from O'Hare Airport. And then there was relief pitcher Oscar Zamora. At the time the Cubs were still playing all day games, which meant the players had their nights free. Oscar liked to spend his evenings sampling Chicago's nightlife. So Oscar told then pitching coach, Marv Grissom, that if he came to the ballpark and his eyes were a little puffy, it was not that he had been out the night before, but it was the "ozones."

I was not sure at the beginning of my time with the Cubs what exactly I was supposed to do, but I knew I had been traded for one of the most beloved of all Cubs, Ron Santo, a man who now does the radio broadcasts for the team. It was an interesting deal. Santo went to the White Sox and I went to the Cubs along with Ken Frailing, Jim Kremmel and Steve Swisher, essentially three minor league players. I like to describe that deal as a trade that hurt both clubs.

My first manager with the Cubs was Whitey Lockman. Whitey's claim to fame as a manger was the fact that he couldn't communicate well with his players. Don't get me wrong, Whitey is a good scout and knows baseball, but he couldn't communicate to the players themselves. Most of your great managers today are excellent communicators, but in 1974, that didn't seem so important. Our third base coach at the time, Jim Marshall, ultimately replaced Whitey as manager.

My three years with the Cubs followed the pattern of my career. I had a few good games, a few bad games. But in the spring of 1975, I wasn't sure if I was

♦

going to have a starting job for the season. I knew it was going to come down to a battle between Ray Burris and me for the one remaining spot.

Ray Burris, at the time, was the second coming of Bob Gibson—tall, a good arm and good control. The Cubs were looking for a big starting pitcher, a situation I had faced many times in my career. My few starts in 1974 put me a notch ahead of Ray going into spring training, but my size and mediocre performances loomed in the background. The other man in the picture was Burt Hooton, the number one draft choice of the Cubs, who had pitched a no-hitter in only his fourth career start back in 1972. Burt's money pitch was his great knuckle-curve and it looked like he was going to be a starter for sure. The first two spots in the rotation were held down by Rick Reuschel, who was a mainstay in the starting rotation for the Cubs in 1975, and Bill Bonham, a young pitcher with great promise. Usually managers are hesitant to go with five starters for the first few months of the season because there are more rain outs and off days. So, with only four spots open, I found myself in a real battle in 1975.

The first start of spring training saw me throw a great three innings, and Ray throw a great three. The second start, I threw a good three and he threw a great three. The third start saw Ray suddenly move ahead of me. He threw a great four innings and I threw a mediocre two. By the fourth start, Ray was allowed to go six. He threw a great six innings and I responded with another mediocre two. As spring went along, it became evident that Ray was going to be their starter. The opening rotation looked like Rick as the number one starter, Bill the number two starter, Burt number three, and Ray number four, with me in the bullpen.

I was very, very down leaving that spring training of 1975, wondering if I would ever get a start, and when that start would be.

◆

My break in 1975 came on opening day. Rick was scheduled to have the honor of starting the opening game, but he came down with the flu. As a result, Bill Bonham got the start. Burt Hooton pitched the second day; Ray Burris pitched the third. On the fourth day, Montreal came to town and Rick Reuschel was scheduled to pitch. As luck would have it, Rick was still too ill to pitch. So I got a start that fourth day, and shut out Montreal, giving up only four hits. We won the game seven to nothing. An impressive performance for a man who was supposed to be in the bullpen at the start of the season.

Jim Marshall had to continue to start me. My next start was against Tom Seaver in New York. I had a good ballgame, pitching into the eighth inning, and beating the Mets, and Tom Terrific, three to one. Even better than the win was the fact that I got a base hit off Tom Seaver, which, for me, was an even more Herculean feat than actually beating him. Now, I'd pushed my record to two wins and no defeats.

I got another start, this one coming against the Philadelphia Phillies in Chicago. Jim Lonborg was my opponent, a man who had prompted teams to put "no skiing" clauses in players' contracts. I threw another complete game and beat him four to one. At 3–0, I suddenly became firmly entrenched in the starting rotation.

As a sidenote, I was one of those players affected by the "no skiing" clause. The "no-skiing" clause came about when Jim Lonborg, at the time a promising young player, took off to ski during the off-season. Like many others do on the slopes, Jim ended up getting hurt. His inability to play at the start of the season prompted the powers that be to insure that such a thing not happen again. In my contract, in addition to skiing, I was barred from motorcycling, hand gliding, and parachuting, none of which I had any inclination to do.

◆

I ran my record to 5–0 before I suffered a hip injury. While favoring my hip I ultimately hurt my arm. At the end of the season the balance sheet read 12–8. Not a great season, but decent.

A comparison of our top two pitchers that year, Rick Reuschel and Bill Bonham, is a study in contrasts. Both men were friends of mine, but Bill, being a more talkative person by nature, seemed to be a closer friend at the time. Certainly, Bill and I shared many an evening discussing a variety of subjects, including what it took to play in the major leagues.

In analyzing these two pitchers, if you put them side by side, Bill would have been a little taller than Rick Reuschel, and a lot leaner and harder. He had a great arm and threw the ball exceptionally hard, consistently ninety-two, ninety-three miles an hour. Bill had a great slider and one of the great change-ups in the National League. At the time a lot of people felt Andy Messersmith owned the best change-up, but Bill's wasn't too far behind.

Rick Reuschel, on the other hand, didn't throw as hard as Bill Bonham and didn't have nearly the pitch selection Bill Bonham had. Neither did he seem to work as hard as Bill Bonham, although, at the time I couldn't tell you anyone who worked as hard as Bill did. Rick threw a sinking fastball and a kind of a roundhouse combination of a slider and a curveball that now has become known as a slurve.

Extracting the physical attributes of both these guys, then, you would have to say that Bill Bonham was the better pitcher. However, the one thing that separated the two of them was the fact that Rick Reuschel truly believed he was going to win. He was fearless on the mound. On the other hand, Bill Bonham was a little more sensitive and insecure. This showed in tough situations. While Rick kept a consistent level of performance, Bill would eventually throw a wild pitch or make a bad throw on a ground ball

♦

73

back to him. Although he was a very good pitcher as far as talent was concerned, Bill never achieved what Rick did in his career because I don't think Bill believed in himself as much as Rick Reuschel did.

Bill was smart enough to realize that if he worked very hard his body would be in great shape. From the sidelines, any coach would say, "This man has got to be a twenty-game winner." Yet, although he had a couple of decent years, he never achieved the long, great career he had hoped for. I think Bill would be the first to admit that this general insecurity as far as his performance was concerned accounted for this lack-luster showing. Bill could never shake the feeling that in a big situation, he wasn't going to get the job done. Eventually this insecurity did him in. At the time, neither Bill nor I could harness our natural ability.

As I approached the 1976 season, I was filled with optimism. After coming off a good year, it's easy to see the possibilities. But at the beginning of the 1976 season, we had a lockout, one of those experiences that people now are all-too-familiar with. The players tried to work out on their own, but it's impossible to keep the skills as honed individually as it is in an organized situation. We had a very short spring training that year which eventually, I believe, caused me to hurt my shoulder.

That year was also unique because I became the first player in the history of the Chicago Cubs to play the entire season without a contract. That was the first year that players were eligible for free agency and I would have been a reluctant free agent. It became a tenuous situation for me because of my arm injury. That year, 1976, was the greatest year of insecurity I had ever experienced. About halfway through the season, I could pitch no longer.

The Cub doctors were of little help, they couldn't diagnose what I had. Finally, I found Dr. Tom Sattler, a kinesthesiologist, a specialist in muscular and bone movement as it relates to athletic performance. I described my symptoms to Tom, and he took me into a room where he had weights and a universal gym. He had me hold my arm out, palm up, and put a one pound weight in my hand. It immediately dropped to the floor. After a few more trys at the weights and a few more exercises, he said, "I know what you have —a rotator cuff injury." At the time, no one had ever heard of a rotator cuff.

The problem the other doctors were having in their diagnoses was the fact that the pains in my arm seemed to move around. Tom explained that four muscles are involved in the rotator and the classic symptom of an injury to it is the movement of pain.

He prescribed a treatment of cryotherapy, a pattern of using ice to freeze the area then going through a series of exercises. The icing of an affected area on the body will increase the blood flow to it enabling the body to heal. Eventually that was exactly what happened. After three months, my shoulder was back to normal. Physically I came back, but the insecurities remained.

There I was in the middle of the 1976 season, a player without a contract, eligible for free agency, and injured. And the Cubs organization was offering me little reassurance. True to form, I met the organization's expectations. My performance faded back to mediocrity. There was no physical reason for me not to pitch in top form, but mentally I had a dozen excuses.

Other people's ability to affect our performance is not limited to baseball. You can see it in yourself. We live up to expectations, and when we let someone else decide the expectations, and they are below our true level of competence, we descend to what is expected of us. In the end, this negative input is programming our failure.

Put it in perspective in your own life. You have a job. You perform adequately, but your boss never asks

♦

your opinion on a new issue, never gives your performance a stretch, overlooks you when something particularly difficult or out of the normal range of performance comes up. For whatever reason, he feels you are not up to the task.

And what do you do? You validate his opinions by giving just enough to satisfy what he expects from you. You become angry because you are consistently passed over and refuse to give that extra effort for someone who obviously doesn't appreciate it, even though the extra effort might change your boss's mind about you. It becomes a vicious circle in which nobody wins and you could ultimately become the big loser because, in time, your own expectations decline.

We must find a way to erase these negatives from our minds and turn our performance around.

In past chapters we used pen and pencil to visually reinforce our positives. Your list of goals should still be your bookmark and your list of positives should be within reach. The physical act of writing this information down and seeing these things in front of us is an excellent method to support our strengthening self-image. Eliminating the negatives needs the same support. Rather than write the negatives down on paper, which would give them a semblance of reality, we are going to only imagine them. Then we'll erase them forever.

Lay back and relax. Close your eyes. Drift into that meditative state we spoke about. If you've been practicing the techniques, already you feel better about yourself whenever you let your mind and body reach to that plateau.

Imagine a blackboard. Make it a huge one. Give yourself plenty of chalk and erasers. What we're going to do is examine those negatives that have embedded themselves in our subconscious, preventing us from reaching our goals. So, now, visualize yourself writing one of those negatives down.

♦

For me, it could have been "I am not strong enough to start thirty-five times and be a consistent winner." For you it could be "I am not as smart as Joe, so I will not get the promotion at work." Or perhaps, "I will never have enough money to afford that new car." Our negative could even be something less materialistic such as "My brother and I always fight, we'll never get along."

You see what we're doing. We're writing down all of the negative beliefs about ourselves that prevent us from not only reaching our goals, but from even *trying* to reach them.

Be careful here to cover only those negative beliefs about yourself and not to list a real obstacle. For example, "I will never have enough money to afford that new car" is a negative belief. "The bank will not make a $20,000 loan on my salary with my current debt" is an obstacle. Obstacles are measurable and capable of being overcome. Negative beliefs are attitudes which prevent us from action.

So let's get back to the blackboard. Look at that first negative belief you've written. Examine it. What made you write it? As I looked at mine, "I am not strong enough to start thirty-five times and be a consistent winner," the memory of that day in San Francisco came back to me. What made me think I wasn't a good enough pitcher when I could remember myself pitching so well? First, the manager was telling me I wasn't a good enough pitcher. I was in the bullpen, not in the starting rotation. I had a losing record. If I were a starter, I'd have a winning record. Over the years, injuries had taken the edge off my game. I had a list of justifications for that negative belief.

As I stared at that blackboard, making my excuses, the smell of new mown grass crept into my subconscious. No matter what reason I came up with to justify that negative belief, there was a nagging

♦
77

thought in my mind that the justification simply wasn't true. I was forced to examine my excuses. "If I were a good enough pitcher, I'd have a winning record, and I don't." That was true, but why didn't I have that winning record. I had to look to myself. And what I saw, I didn't like.

Over the years, I had some great games. But for every great game I had, there were many more that were mediocre. At the time, I even justified those poor performances with excuses. The manager took me out of the game too early. I just won two in a row, I'm due for a few losses. After all, nobody wins all the time. Who can win in Yankee Stadium with that short right field wall and a lineup of left-handed hitters? A graveyard for right-handed pitchers, to be sure, and I was a right-hander. I let my mind wander to those losing moments. I visualized myself on the mound and let myself remember.

At each and every failure, I found that I had some excuse, someone or something to blame for not winning. And never was that someone responsible for my failure ever me. Sound familiar? My poor performance in Yankee Stadium was not due to a short right field wall. Give me a break. If that were true, every right-handed pitcher would lose every time at Yankee Stadium. My poor performance was due to the fact that I went into each and every game in Yankee Stadium convinced I was not going to win it.

No wonder the managers put me in the bullpen. I certainly was not as consistently valuable to the team as those guys who could be counted on to perform game after game. It was almost like I was saying to them and myself, "Okay, if you don't think I'm that valuable to the team, I won't be."

And the injuries, not even those could be used as an excuse.

In 1976, after I suffered my rotator cuff injury, the Cubs let me go to free agency. My worst nightmare

♦

was coming true. Fortunately, in 1977, Bill Veeck gave me the opportunity to get back into baseball and play for the White Sox. So, there I was stumbling along in spring training, trying to find my way, and really trying to protect against another arm injury. The physical effects of my injury were long past, but the psychological effects lingered. Every time I threw the ball I hedged. I wondered with every pitch if it would be the one to damage my shoulder again. I wasn't pitching well at all and I was sinking deeper and deeper into Bob Lemon's dog house.

Bob Lemon's frustration with me was nothing compared to my frustration with myself. I knew I was failing, but the nagging fear of injury stayed with me. I looked back on my career, starting with my early illness during my Cape Cod season, and blamed whatever forces were responsible for my illnesses and injuries for my lack of performance. It wasn't right. It wasn't fair. And it wasn't my fault that I had to suffer through this series of misfortunes.

As was his custom, my father came down to see me in spring training. I was not doing well and certainly would have preferred my father not to have to witness what I was going through. But he had been right behind me since I was a child and there was no way I was going to stop him from coming to see me now.

It was my fifth outing, late in the spring. We were playing the Cincinnati Reds. This game was going no better than any of the others. I had given up half a dozen or more hits, one home run to Ray Knight who, at the time, was a budding young third baseman for the Reds. By the fifth inning my nerves were strung out. My curveball, the foundation of my game, had failed me. My fastball wasn't even worth the effort. My frustrations for an entire spring training were building to a peak in this one game.

It was the bottom of the fifth, what I knew would be my last inning for this game. The Reds had two

◆

outs and I was facing the pitcher. What was happening to me? I could strike this guy out. I knew it. I just had to do it. I channeled every bit of energy I had into my arm. You've been there. You'll become so mad with yourself, you simply act, seemingly without thought. That's where I was. I forgot about why I couldn't and just did.

I lined up and threw a curve. YES! He swung and missed. I can do it I kept telling myself. I threw another curve that went just inside the plate. Ball one. Calm down. Set your sights. I set up for a fastball. Reason was beginning to return. He fouled it off. I felt my focus coming back. I threw another fastball that was just outside. At any other point in spring training my heart would have been racing. I would have been thinking of the hundreds of things that could go wrong with the next pitch. I would have been conscious of my arm. But not this time. I looked down to the ground and inhaled. I knew what I had to do. I could feel it—in my mind, in my legs, in my arm. Nothing else mattered except the next pitch. I threw the ball as hard as I could. He swung. Strike three.

I came off the mound and met Bob Lemon in the dugout. "There it is," he said to me. "You threw the ball. I've been waiting all spring for you to throw the ball."

There was nothing I could say.

That night I had dinner with my father. He was usually pretty talkative, but that evening he was quiet. Finally, when we had finished eating, I said, "Dad, is something wrong? Something you're not telling me?"

"I was just going to ask you the same thing. What is wrong?"

I pretended that I didn't know what he was talking about.

"Steve, I've been watching you play since you were six. You have always given the game as much as you had, but not now. How come? Is this not what you want to do any more?"

I shrugged. "It's my shoulder. I just don't want to hurt it again."

He nodded as if agreeing. "So it's still bothering you then?"

"No," I said, "It's just that I don't want to risk, you know . . ."

At that point he leaned across the table. "You don't want to risk what? You tell me your shoulder's fine, then pitch like your shoulder's fine. Let's face it, you're not a kid anymore. There's more of your career behind you then in front of you. If you still want to play in the major leagues, then you're going to have to play at the top of your game."

"But, Dad," I started to argue, "I can't risk throwing my shoulder in spring training. I have to save it for . . ."

"Save it for what? You don't pitch like a winner in training, nobody is going to give you a chance to pitch during the season. What's the worst thing that can happen? You throw the ball, your arm falls off. Then you have to do something else. Someday you're going to have to do something else anyway. Might as well have to make that decision knowing you went out fighting instead of just giving up." He leaned back in his chair and gave me one of those smiles he used to give me when I was a kid. The kind of smile every parent gives their child when they know they've just won the argument.

"You're right," I admitted, "I can't keep going the way I'm going. The shoulder's fine. I just have to *believe* the shoulder will hold up. I know someday that I'll have to do something else rather than play ball, but right now I'm not ready to do that. I still have it in me to play. And I still have it in me to win. I have to remember that when I go out there and just pitch."

◆

"You will, Steve," he said as he rose from the chair. "Now pay the check."

We can convince ourselves of anything and, at that point in my career, I had let myself believe that I had lost the ability to win. My conscious mind denied it, of course, but my subconscious was convinced that I was not a good enough pitcher to remain in the majors. I went back to training and stopped protecting the arm. My level of performance raised and Bob Lemon used me as a starter that season. His confidence in me helped me develop confidence in myself.

As I said, I had a pretty good season that year. It wasn't until 1979, though, when Earl Weaver confronted me, that I had to face the fact that Bob Lemon's confidence in me was more responsible for my success than my belief in myself. In 1979, I looked at my mental blackboard. "I am not a strong enough pitcher to start thirty-five times and win consistently." That year, I was able to say, "No that is not true. I am a good enough pitcher to carry the late innings. I am a good enough pitcher to start. I am a good enough pitcher to win."

I erased that negative belief from my mind.

You must do the same thing. You have to analyze those negative inputs and discover where they came from. Were they put there by someone else? Or did you do it? Most of all, you have to ask yourself "Do I believe this?" After you have studied what you have written, you must confront it. Why is this not true? It is not true because you are good enough to get that promotion. Because you can learn anything you set your mind to. Because you can pitch and win in the seventh, eighth, and ninth innings.

Now erase your negatives. Mentally pick up that eraser and wipe each negative off the board. Watch yourself eliminating those inputs from your life. Once it's done, you will no longer allow those negatives to prevent you from reaching your goal. No longer will

♦

these be blockades to the success you want. Everyone of them is now gone. Your blackboard is clean, as if nothing had ever been written on it.

Once you've gotten rid of those negatives, you have to prevent them from returning. To do this, you have to build a wall around yourself, one that filters out the minuses that can seep in and rewrite what you have just eliminated. One way to protect this state of mind is to imagine a positive cocoon around you which repels negatives and emphasizes positives. Visualize it as mental armor bouncing away anything which threatens your success and absorbing those things which help you grow. In 1979, I began building my cocoon; it wasn't easy. I had to work at it, even to the point of making myself visualize it every time I went out to pitch. My first real test of this cocoon, though, came against my old nemesis, the New York Yankees.

Starting with a two-game series in 1973, through 1977, 1978, and 1979, I never beat the Yankees. As I said, I could guarantee I was going to lose to them simply because I had set myself up to lose. There may have been dozens of negatives buried in my subconscious about my being able to pitch in general, but my losing to the Yankees was a specifically defined failure. So I can tell you, the big negative written on my blackboard in the late summer of 1980 was "I cannot beat the Yankees in Yankee Stadium."

Since the All-Star break of 1979, I had been using the meditation and visualization techniques quite successfully. I knew that my mental preparation was the reason for my growing success, but up to this Yankee game, I hadn't faced a team with which I had so much negative, emotional luggage. And I was facing them on their own turf. I tried, like every athlete engaged in competition, to take it one game at a time, but the Yankee game loomed larger than life on the schedule.

♦

In the early season, I had taken my first win from the Yankees. On June 12, 1980, at Baltimore, I finally broke my streak. That game had been difficult to face, but I had the home field advantage and it was early enough in the season not to have been a critical game for the Orioles. By August, the pennant race had tightened. We were scheduled for eight games against the Yankees, three at their park and five at ours, with only a series against Kansas City in between. We had to take at least six of the eight to have a shot at the pennant.

The importance of this first part of the series coupled with a packed house of 55,000 New York fans was overwhelming. The bullpen mound in Yankee Stadium is out by the old monuments. As I stared at those great names in Yankee history, my focus sharpened. I had not lost a game since the All-Star break. I told myself I was not due to lose one now. I had never beaten the Yankees. Now was the time to start. I finished my warm-ups, all the while clearing my mind of negatives. By the time I took the field, I was never more ready for a game. I finally realized that no matter what had happened between me and the Yankees in 1973 or 1977 or 1978 or 1979, it could not affect me this day, unless I let it. And I was not about to. I concentrated and delivered the first pitch. A perfect curve. A strike.

I went on to finish that game and beat them four to two. Four games later I came back and pitched a two hitter and beat them six to one in our park. Just as the early San Francisco Giants batting practice had taught me how good I could be, that first game in Yankee Stadium taught me that I did not have to live on past failures. I could win. Oscar Wilde said, "Success is a science; if you have the conditions, you get the result." I say you can control the conditions.

Now that you see how negatives can build up and how difficult they are to erase, I'm going to give you a list of twenty-five phrases you can never use again.

◆

1. I tried that before and it didn't work.
2. It may have worked for you, my situation is different.
3. I'd like to but I just don't have the time.
4. My family/friends/boss will never accept it.
5. It's against the rules.
6. It won't make a difference in the long run.
7. Let's see what tomorrow brings.
8. I can't plan that far in advance.
9. It sounds good in theory but. . . .
10. I'm too old/young/middle-aged.
11. It costs too much.
12. I've already decided against it.
13. Things are just fine the way they are.
14. People will think I'm crazy.
15. I can't do everything.
16. It's too much trouble.
17. I need guarantees.
18. I've run out of ideas.
19. If I could just see it in action.
20. When things settle down, I'll take a look at it.
21. I have everything I need.
22. I'm too tired.
23. I don't want to commit.
24. I don't want to be the first.
25. It can't be done.

Every time you start a thought or begin an action with one of the above phrases you can be guaranteed of not succeeding. Using them is like preprogramming negatives, so whenever you catch yourself saying them, or even thinking them, erase the thought and begin again. Consciously throw the negative out of your mind. Regroup. Rephrase. Restart.

Now let's get back to the goals. If the goals are real and not fantasy, we are looking at things that are achievable and, more than likely, successful extensions of what we are doing now. One of your goals, I would venture to guess, involves your career. Perhaps it is a better job or higher pay.

On the surface, we all claim to be doing our jobs, and, most of the time, we claim to be doing them well. For many of us this is probably true, for if we weren't doing them at least adequately, we would be fired. But the question I put to you is, are you doing your job as well as it can be done? Or at least as well as you can do it? Be honest. The answer is probably not.

I knew I wasn't performing as well as I could have been as a pitcher. Sure, you say, you were a pitcher in the major leagues, so how bad could you have been? Yes, I pitched for some great teams, and I pitched for some mediocre ones. I even had spurts of brilliance, but the truthful answer is that I performed at a level that was enough to get by, to win enough games to have guaranteed starts, to have a contract the following spring. I performed at a level expected of me by my bosses and let that level become what I expected of myself. When Earl Weaver called me on the level of my performance, my immediate response was that I had performed to a level required of me before, so what was his problem now.

I am not unique. I know that you perform to the level that is expected of you at your job. If you are supposed to make ten sales calls in one week, the standard specified for your job, then ten sales calls is what you make. If your job is to see that end of the month reports come out of the computer on the tenth working day of the following month, on the tenth day the boss gets them. If your hours are from eight to five, you are always there on time and leave pretty close to five. I've even heard people boast of the fact that they are entitled to one sick day a month, and they never use more than that. If this is your behavior, are you performing to the level expected of your job? Technically, yes. Are you performing your job well? No.

Job expectations are important to know. They tell us the standards to which our employers hold us. Supposedly they prevent favoritism and discrimination. They give us direction and focus. However, the very nature of defining performance is dangerous. It can damage our employer by hampering creativity and, more importantly, harm us by limiting our goals.

When I was a rookie, I had all the enthusiasm and energy of anyone beginning a new job. I knew I was more fortunate than most in that I was doing something I loved to do, but that same exuberance comes over most of us when we start a new task. I worked my way steadily up the league ladder, learning my craft, putting my own personality into the task I had to perform, learning the little tricks of the job just like anyone else in any trade. But there came a point, and I'm not sure just when that was, when the level of my performance became secondary to just getting the job done. At that point in time, my goal changed from being the best pitcher I could be to simply winning the next game. My performance record said I was a .500 pitcher at best and I believed it. Don't get me wrong, I still loved my job, but my focus changed from what I wanted to be as a pitcher to what my manager, the team, and the fans expected of me. And, I am willing to bet, the same thing has happened to you in your careers.

Do you go to work each day thinking about those things you must get done? Sure, we all do. The real question, though, is do you think about these tasks as output which must be done correctly and on a timely basis, or do you think about goals that must be achieved? For example, those ten sales calls you have to make, are ten sales calls the goal or is one new account the true measure of success?

Let's take a look at that more closely. Your company says that if you get an order from one out of ten calls, the company will make money and you are doing your job well. So the sales department in the home office defines the level of performance expected as ten sales calls a week. Perhaps the requirement of ten sales calls a week was not the most effective way of communicating the true goal of sales performance, but many times, inadequate communication is a stumbling block to us all. Pretty soon, a whole bureaucracy is formed around monitoring who makes ten sales calls and who doesn't. What do you do as a salesperson out in the field, you set up a schedule which allows you to stop at ten different places each week. Only secondary to this schedule is the consideration of how successful each call will be. In this scenario, nobody wins.

As a field salesperson, you have to ask yourself, what is your goal. Being the person you are, striving to be successful, you say your goal is to sell $10,000 a week of your company's product. This has nothing to do with how many calls you make. Your next step is to detail those customers who will most likely translate into a sale. The right thing to do is to spend your time cultivating their business. So, the first week goes by and you only make six calls, but of the six, three are successful. Have you met the company standards? I think so.

The next thing you will say to me is that, whether or not your sales quota has been exceeded, those clowns back in the home office want ten sales calls, and if they don't get their ten, you're in trouble. Perhaps that might be true if you made six calls and none were successful, but that is unlikely because you've spent your time culling out the losers and focusing on the winners. The ball is in your court, then, to have them reevaluate. I would venture to say that if you brought up the subject to the home office in terms of what the true goal really is, and proved it through your own successful performance, you would see some changes. At that point, they would have to

♦

look again and see that the number of calls is not the objective, sales made is.

Look what you've done for yourself. First, you have met the sales dollar quota and probably exceeded it. Secondly, you have improved the manner in which your company evaluates its standard of performance to focus not on the level of activity but on the level of success. Third, you have done something productive and meaningful allowing you to take pride in your own performance. Lastly, you have impressed your bosses. They will remember it.

This sounds simplistic, and it is. The concept, though, of superior performance merely being mediocre, isn't. John Teets, Chairman of the Greyhound-Dial Corporation, imparts the belief in this philosophy to his employees regularly. "Business needs to focus their attention on people productivity, and that means every individual working to his or her fullest potential. Efficiency can become mediocrity. There is always room for improvement and growth no matter what your job or how long you've been in the same position. It is up to you to strive to become better. The company cannot do it for you. You are responsible for setting goals and challenges for yourself."

Sound familiar?

I admit that when I signed with the Orioles I felt everyone was working against me, the team, the fans, Earl—most especially, Earl. But that, of course, wasn't true, as I began to find out one day, early in my tenure with the Orioles, after a particularly frustrating game. One, which needless to say, I lost.

I was showering in the locker room, having left the field without saying a word to anyone. I had been taken out about the middle of the game and, in my mind, I blamed Earl for taking me out too early, thinking I might have won if I stayed in longer. I blamed my shoulder, which seemed to act up in direct proportion to how poorly I was pitching. I blamed the

♦

fans, who had made their preference for other pitchers on the staff clear. I had a list of people and things I was ready to blame as I let the water run over me.

A few days earlier there had been an article in the paper about the crazy things players get in their contracts, private rooms on the road, incentives, limos. One of the things highlighted in this article was my Cy Young Award clause, a $10,000 bonus if I won. This was listed as one of the more ridiculous. Here was a pitcher with a 67–72 lifetime record with a clause like that in his contract. They laughed at that one. Standing in the shower, I snickered too.

Just as I was ready to lay the blame on the newspaper writer, Terry Crowley, a pinch hitter, came up behind me, in uniform, spikes and all. "We know where you came from, second division teams," he said. "Let me tell you this, bad teams give the game away in the seventh, eighth, and ninth innings. We take away the game in those innings. That's why it's important to you to pitch long into the game. We don't score early and we don't kill teams but we beat teams in the seventh, eighth, and ninth innings."

I turned to answer him, tell him something like, "I'd love to but Earl never lets me stay that long," but by the time I turned off the water, Terry was gone.

The next week, Earl did it to me again. It was a home game against the Toronto Blue Jays and I was losing it about mid-game. One of the cardinal rules in baseball is that the pitcher waits on the mound for the manager to come out to him. Earl loved this rule. It let him march out to midfield and point to the bullpen with all the drama of a Shakespearean play and take me out of the game. But this time I was having none of it. In my mind, it was Earl Weaver's fault I was losing the game. If he only let me stay in until the last inning, I would win. Instead of waiting, I started to walk right toward him, flipping the ball into his hands as I walked to the dugout. I did not even make it to the

◆

As a member of the
Brush High School
baseball team, I wasn't
the biggest, but no one
tried harder.

At Kent State I always felt all the
scouts were there to see Thurman
Munson. It wasn't until later that I
realized that I was using this as an
excuse when I did poorly.

My first major league victory brought this congratulatory telegram from
my old friend and teammate Thurman Munson.

western union   Telegram

```
                                    1971 APR 24  PM 7  33
    623P EST APR 24 71 PA421 SYA436
    SY NB146 XNTO387 DS CGN PDF NEW YORK CITY NY 24 1013A EST
    STEVE STONE, SAN FRANCISCO GIANTS, DLY 75
       PITTSBURGH STADIUM PGH
    CONGRATULATIONS ON YOUR FIRST VICTORY
       THURMAN MUNSUN NEW YORK YANKEES.

    (1210)
```

I was lucky enough to play for both of the Chicago baseball teams during my career.

With my father, Paul, in
Sarasota during my first spring
training with the Chicago White
Sox, 1973.

A prelude of things to come — Harry Caray interviews
me in old Comiskey Park in 1973.

I'm not sure if any amount of visualization
could have helped this career .100 hitter.
Thankfully I was rescued by the desig-
nated hitter rule.

After years of being not too bad, not too good, 1980 saw me become a focused, determined winner.

The two starting pitchers for the 1980 All-Star game, J.R. Richards and I, enjoy a laugh during the All-Star luncheon.

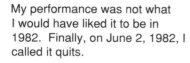

No matter how good my preparation, it wouldn't make any difference if my shoulder was hurting. Here Ralph Salvon, former Baltimore trainer, does some work on my shoulder.

My performance was not what I would have liked it to be in 1982. Finally, on June 2, 1982, I called it quits.

One way to ensure success in business is to get everyone involved in every aspect of a business – including the owner.

My other broadcast partner, when Harry moves over to the radio side, is Thom Brennaman.

No, I don't always wear a tuxedo in the booth, but this was a special night. Bill Murray joins the festivities for the first night game in Wrigley Field history, 8-8-88.

Harry Caray, the greatest spokesman baseball has ever seen, and yours truly from our familiar perch in Wrigley Field.

It is not easy to try and replace a legend, but that is exactly what WGN was faced with when Harry Caray had his stroke. Here are a few of the men who kept Harry's seat warm in his absence. LEFT, George Will.

Dick Enberg

Jim Belushi

Ernie Harwell

shower before Earl confronted me and we had another one of our season long shouting matches.

"You tried to show me up out there," Earl's face was crimson and saliva was coming out the corners of his mouth, "and nobody, get it, nobody shows me up out there. I've been here twelve years, and my record says I'm a great manager. What does your record say? I'm a smart man, you may not think so, but I am. When I say it's time for you to come out, you don't know best, I do. So I'm telling you this, if I ever get the chance to show you up, I will. Remember that, I will."

This time it was Lee May who came up behind me in the shower. "You ever notice when you played against us, we seemed to get lucky in the late innings?" he asked me. "We never beat you big, but we always seemed to get that lucky base hit in the eighth. You know why? It's because we know how to stick in there and win. And if you want to be part of that, you've got to stick in there and win." With that, he walked away.

Earl got his chance to make good on his threat two days later. It was the last game before the All-Star break of 1979. Jim Palmer was scheduled to pitch, but he couldn't. I had a lot of success against the California Angels, but my normal rest period between games was three days, and with Baltimore, I had gotten used to four or five days in between games. My arm was pretty weak, but there was no one else available, so I agreed to pitch the game.

In the third inning I gave up a tremendous home run to Don Baylor and by the sixth inning, when I gave up another couple of runs, I was getting exhausted. I told Ray Miller I needed to get out, but Earl kept me in the game. "That's what you want, to stay in the game, that's what you'll get."

The seventh inning started with a ringing double. Bobby Grich came up next and hit a home run high off the left field foul pole. I retired the next hitter, which brought up Don Baylor. Baylor already had one home run, and I shouldn't have been facing him again, but Earl had to prove his point. Well Don walloped one even farther into left field than Bobby Grich. Before the game ended, I heard someone comment that the hitters moved the big "A" which was emblazoned out in left field, just a little farther back.

This time it was Mark Belanger who confronted me in the shower. I can tell you, I was getting a little annoyed at being told off stark naked and wet. "We are winners in Baltimore," he said. "We know we're winners. Your job is to keep us close enough in the beginning, the middle, and the end, so we can keep on being winners."

They were telling me their secret, why Baltimore for the longest time had the most wins in the major leagues. It was the attitude "We are winners, we can do it," and the whole team had it. Individuals who came to the team were expected to pick this attitude up, or move on. Their strategy was simple. All they had to do was keep themselves in a position to win, to avail themselves of any opportunity that came along. If the competition didn't give them an opportunity, they created one for themselves. Every team got the same breaks, that's the law of averages, but not every team was close enough to take advantage of that luck, for lack of a better word, to convert an opportunity into a win. They didn't make mistakes. They were constantly alert.

At that moment, though, I had other things on my mind. I still had to contend with Earl. The smug sense of satisfaction he had plastered on his face infuriated me. Instead of using sound baseball sense, which is what he used to explain his reasons for taking me out early, he used unsound baseball sense to teach me a lesson. I was ready for war, but Ray Miller had had enough. It was then that he called the fateful meeting between Earl and myself that ultimately served to turn my career around. And it was after that meeting that I finally understood what Terry, Lee, and Mark were trying to tell me. You have to be prepared to win, all the time.

The same principles my teammates spoke of can be applied to anyone who works for a living. Those lucky breaks you always accuse everyone else of getting come your way, too, but if you're not in a position to take advantage of them, you let them slide on by. If that happens to you often enough, you won't even recognize them as they pass you over for someone else. Pretty soon, the mediocrity will turn to boredom then to frustration and bitterness.

This is why it is critical to remain fresh and self-challenged. Every one *can* be a winner. There is enough success to go around. Not only can everyone be a winner, everyone is *entitled* to be a winner.

That's something. Not only can you be a success, you deserve it.

6

Keeping Concentration

As I said, when I was a rookie, I had all the enthusiasm and energy needed to play at top form. One thing I lacked, however, was the concentration I needed to compete in the major leagues. Up until my rookie year, I always seemed to be able to keep my mind in focus, but that year something happened. I was like a kid in a candy shop, too excited to be able to get down to the business of deciding what I wanted.

A perfect example of this was my first outing in Shea Stadium. New York fans had packed the stands to see *the* Willie Mays. New York was where he started and there's nothing to beat the loyalty and intensity of New York fans (except, perhaps, that of the Cubs' fans).

◆

I have to admit I was in awe. Here I was, twenty-three years old, starting a game in front of 55,000 fans in Shea Stadium. A standing room only crowd to see the Giants play the Mets. Getting ready and going out to pitch a baseball game is one thing. For the most part, I would pour my energy into preparing for the game. I would think about the opposing team, and try to develop some sort of strategy for each opposing batter. Some days I did this more intensely than others, but, for every game, the process was pretty much the same. However, this day in New York with the stadium packed was something else entirely.

I remember walking onto the field, feeling all those eyes on me. "They're here to see Willie," I told myself as I approached the mound. There is an unreal quality to the sound of a crowd when you're below them on a baseball field. You know the decibel level is high, but there is an echoing sensation which melds all the different noises into one. I'm not sure whether you actually hear the fans or whether you just think you hear them. Anyway, as a twenty-three-year-old rookie, I can tell you, that day, I heard each and every one of them.

As I stood on the mound and listened to the crowd cheer for Willie Mays, I thought to myself how great it would be if all these fans had come to see me. I looked toward the stands, then it occurred to me that this is exactly what happened. They did come to see me, only no one realized that but me. "I'm in control," I thought to myself. "If I don't throw the ball, nobody's going to see a baseball game. Wouldn't it be interesting if I just stood here with the ball in my hand? I wonder what would happen if I didn't throw it? Who would get to see Willie Mays then?"

Impressive preparation wouldn't you say? I distracted myself enough on the mound before the game to lose that day. As a matter of fact, I let myself get distracted often enough during my rookie year that I would up 5–9 by the end of it.

In retrospect, some of this distraction was due to the situation. Here I was, after a lifetime of preparation, exactly where I wanted to be, doing exactly what I wanted to do. I had achieved my dream. How many boys start out wanting to grow up to play big league ball? When I was a kid, every other player on any team I was on had the same dream as me. Our heroes were ballplayers. At night we'd sleep with our gloves and ball next to our pillows. We'd talk about the players like we had some inside track to what they were thinking and how they lived. We could see ourselves on the field playing to just the same kind of crowd I faced in Shea Stadium. Who wouldn't have become distracted?

The problem was that my dream was also my job. In order to be a big league player, I had to play baseball, and play to a level above any other I had before. There was no opportunity to just stand out on the field and enjoy the ride, I had to work. I had to work effectively. In order to do this, I had to concentrate. Believe me, concentrating on the task at hand was a major feat.

When I was playing amateur baseball in Cleveland, Ohio, in a Class A city league called the Whenham Truckers, we had a fellow named Lou Konja in the organization. Lou was a former player in the New York Yankees minor league system until he hurt his arm. During his time with the Yankees organization, though, he got to be friendly with Mel Stottlemyre. Mel is now the pitching coach with the New York Mets, and I run into him eighteen times a year, whenever the Cubs play the Mets, but at that point, Mel was a star pitcher with the Yankees, a potent team at the time. They had all the greats, Roger Maris, Mickey Mantle, Joe Pepitone. I was a freshman in college, and, when the Yankees came to town, Lou took me to the game and promised to take me to dinner with Mel Stottlemyre afterwards. For me, this was a real thrill.

Lou was a fairly big fellow at six-foot-four; Mel is a few inches shorter. After the game, the three of us were walking from the ballpark to Lou's car. A young man, maybe twelve, had followed us asking for our autographs. Lou, being a former player, signed the young man's paper. Mel, of course, signed. The boy gave the paper to me and I said, "Son, I'm not a baseball player."

He pushed the paper back to me. "Please, please sign this. You all say that. You all tell me that you're not players, and you are players, and you don't sign and I don't have the autograph."

"Really, I'm not a professional player. I'm just a kid in college along for the ride."

"They all say that. All the time they say that. Just please sign the paper."

I tried to walk away, but he persisted, actually following us from the stadium to Lou's car. Finally, as I was getting into the car, he says, "Look, I don't care who you are, just sign this for me."

Realizing there was no other way out, I calmly took his paper and signed "Best Wishes, Steve Stone."

He took the paper back, looked at it, and said "Oh, who are you?"

We got a good laugh over that in the car, but the incident led into what Mel told me at dinner. I must have drilled Mel with every question a young player could ask of a major leaguer. For five hours, he patiently answered each of my questions never once putting me off. Finally, I said, "Look, guys at this level are getting hits off me, and sometimes getting runs off me. If the guys at this level are doing this, how in the world can I ever think of pitching in the major leagues?"

♦

He looked at me. "What's your best pitch?"

I thought a minute. "I throw the ball pretty hard, but I think my best pitch is a curveball."

At that point, he said "Remember a couple of things. One is you can respect the fellows you're playing against but you can never hold them in awe because it's your job to get them out. If you put them on a pedestal, you can't perform against them. You have to truly believe you are better than they are. That way you can get them out, do your job, make a lot of money, and become famous down the road.

"Remember something else. Nobody hits a good curveball. Not in little league, not in pony league, not in college and not in the major leagues. If you have a good curveball, you get them out.

"So my advice to you is get a good curveball and truly believe you're better than the man you're facing."

Many years later my conversation with Mel came back to me as I was watching a young racquetball player competing for the title in his first state championship. I fancy myself an intense competitor in any situation and, to be quite honest, I hate to lose. The reason that this young player caught my attention at this meet was that he had beaten me three out of four games just two weeks earlier, in a "fun" match. I consider myself a good player, but at seventeen, this kid was magnificent. He was definitely out of my reach.

I happened to be in Maryland around Christmas time and was surprised to see the same young man on the card. He was up against a seasoned thirty-five-year-old player who didn't possess nearly the skill or ability of this young man but had the advantage of being a trained competitor. The older player did everything he could to distract the young man. I mean everything. He would go back, set up, then step on the young man's foot. He would try to push him out. The younger player would hit a sure winner and the older player would complain to one of the referees that the ball skipped. Sometimes the older player would even manage to get a call overturned, but the main objective was simply to disrupt this kid's game. That was the strategy, to keep the younger player off his game plan by forcing him to lose concentration. The strategy was working, because the young man lost the first game fifteen to nine.

By the end of that first game, I was as frustrated as the young man. I knew exactly what was happening and there was nothing I could do about it. Boy, did I want to shake that kid. He had the championship in the bag if he could only pull it off. I recognized the position he was in.

He was losing the second game eleven to three when I saw him call a time-out. Bear in mind, I hardly knew this young man, only having played him once. I wasn't his coach and was only a very good amateur player myself. When I saw him leave the court, though, I had to go downstairs and say something to him. I knew I could help him out.

"You're going to lose to this guy and you really shouldn't," I began, then realized I probably should reintroduce myself before giving advice. "You have far superior ability."

"I know that," the young man said. It was obvious from the expression on his face that even though he knew he possessed better skills, he was at a loss as to how to turn the situation around.

"The reason he's going to beat you," I said, "is that he is making you experience all the wrong emotions at the wrong time. He's taking you out of your game plan by distracting you. And you're letting him."

What was the young man going to say? I was becoming excited. It was almost as if I was out there on the court.

"Do this," I said. "You have the two red serving lines. Give yourself any emotion you want outside the two red lines. You want to yell at the referee, yell at the

♦

99

referee. You want to yell at this guy, yell at this guy. You want to bemoan the fact that you're down in the second game and are well on your way to being eliminated—that's fine. Feel sorry for yourself. Do whatever you want to. But when you go between the red serving lines, focus. Stare at the tiger emblem on your glove. As soon as that tiger becomes crystal clear, as soon as there is nothing else in the world that exists but the head of that tiger, when it has clarified to the point that you see the sharpest image you could ever see, serve the ball. You've made 100,000 serves in your lifetime. Your body knows what to do. Don't let yourself become distracted. You know you can do it."

I could see him evaluate what I was saying. He ran his hand over his glove as if his touch could begin the process.

"What you will do is take all of this diverse energy that you've been wasting, yelling at everybody, bouncing off walls, tripping over this guy, and watching that stupid beanie he's wearing, and turn it into your own power. Wipe away all those excess emotions and turn that energy into a narrow beam of light. When the tiger's head is positively glowing, serve the ball. You know you're better than he is. You know you're faster. You hit the ball harder. All these things will come into play if you wash away all these emotions and get back to business."

And he did. He went back on to the court and before his first serve I watched him stare at the tiger's head on his glove. Then he positioned to serve. He was ready. I could see it in his face. Eventually he won the second game fifteen to fourteen. And he took the third fifteen to three. He was successful because he was able to redirect all his concentration back to a narrow beam of light, focused on the task at hand.

I wish someone would have taught me this back at Shea Stadium. It would have given me many more years of improved performance.

◆

Losing concentration is easy. We do it all the time. Most of us even know when it happens. The problem becomes how to get it back, and quickly.

Many of us lose concentration simply because we think we don't need it. Take a job you've been doing for long enough that you perform it by rote. Do you consider yourself a "paper-pusher"? Well, if you handle a great deal of paperwork at your job and simply run it past your desk, that's what you've made yourself, a "paper-pusher." Bear in mind that losing concentration and not thinking about what you are doing are two different things. When you don't think about the task at hand, you make errors, you have accidents. We pay attention enough to avoid these things. What we need to do is focus our attention on the purpose of the task, on the greater value of our energy. With the end goal in mind, we can concentrate more effectively on the task we are doing.

Let's get back to all that paper you're pushing over your desk. Whether we believe it or not, every piece of paper started out with a purpose. I know enough people who work in offices that to swear to me this isn't so, but at some point in time, somebody thought this information was useful and created a form, a report, or a comment card to record it. I know this is hard to believe, especially if you're the poor person who's job it is to compile, compare, report, and file it. And this is where concentration comes in.

Have you ever really looked at the task you are performing? I'm not talking about looking at it to see if you are performing it correctly or that the person who handed you the information performed whatever they were supposed to do correctly or even if the person you handed it to used it correctly. I'm talking about looking at the meaning of what you are doing.

Do you handle invoices? Do you know what your organization's biggest sellers are? If you read what's on those invoices, you can tell. Do you know who your organization's largest customers are? Again, if you look at who is getting these pieces of paper you're pushing across your desk, you'd be able to tell.

Do you take care of shipping for your company? Where do you sell most of your goods? How do you ship them? How many deliveries don't get there on time?

How many copies of every piece of paper do you produce? Where do they go? Does everyone who gets one use it?

These seem like very basic questions. They are. I bet you even asked yourself these same things or made note of these points at some time or another while doing your job. The point is, though, do you ask yourself these questions every day.

When you first got your position, remember how intensely you paid attention, trying to learn every-thing there was to learn about what you were doing. Two years ago you knew that Mega Corp. was your biggest customer and they bought over $1,000,000 of your product every year. You found that out because you read and paid attention to every piece of paper that came across your desk. When was the last time you did that? Maybe Mega Corp. is buying $2,000,000 now. Or, just maybe, they're buying it from somebody else. Not your job to worry about that? Think again.

Wherever you work, you are part of a team. Perhaps your co-workers don't confront you while you're in the shower like Crowley, May, and Belanger did to me, but, nonetheless, your success affects the success of others. If you don't have a firm grip on where you want to go and how you want to get there, you can kill an entire effort. There may be little cogs in every wheel, but rarely are there unnecessary ones.

I believe that.

I had a restaurant in Scottsdale, Arizona, named Steven. It was a fine dining establishment which prided itself on the best quality food coupled with the

♦

best service available. Over the years, it built a large and loyal customer base.

It was successful for the obvious reasons restaurants are successful, excellent perceived price-value, location, and a well-targeted market. But I feel there was one other reason Steven's was successful. I made a point of letting every employee know how critical each one of them was to the process. Dishwashers had to know more than just how to get plates and silverware clean. Servers had to know the constraints under which chefs operated. As the owner and host, I even bussed a table or two. The entire staff sampled the menu. Not just servers, but dishwashers, utility men, even my accountant tried every dish, and more than once. They had to know what was in it and how it was made. In my mind, it was important that each person who contributed to Steven's success be aware of their role in the process and the roles of others. Without this full knowledge, I saw no way anyone could perform to the best of his ability. And, I felt that only by a continuous reinforcement of this knowledge could the team effort and superior performance these people exhibited be continued.

In my own business, I made it a point to work at letting my people know how important they were to the organization. Because of this, my employees were able to consistently direct their focus to the ultimate task, making Steven successful. I am not naive enough to think, however, that every organization does the same thing. Many do not. While ultimately it is the organization which pays the price for such neglect, the more immediate penalty is paid by the employee in mediocre performance, undefined goals, lack of creativity.

Over the years there have been extraordinary baseball teams. The 1927 Yankees, the Oakland A's of the early 1970s, Cincinnati's "Big Red Machine" of the mid-1970s, and Baltimore of the late 1970s and

♦

early 1980s, but, for the most part, the cumulative skill level of any team's players is fairly consistent. Which means on any given day, any team can beat any other. So why do some teams reach the top regularly and others not? It's not the desire to win because if you ask any player, "do you want to win?" the answer will certainly be yes. Who wants to lose? You can even ask any player, "are you up for winning, excited to win, intense to win?" The answer to that will be yes. There is an intensity that builds before a game that is contagious. So what's the difference?

For one thing, concentration and intensity are not the same thing. Intensity is an integral part of concentration. It must be maintained to constantly be a winner. Without it, the desire to win degenerates and, with it, performance. But it is only a part of what is needed for concentration. The missing ingredient which differentiates the two is focus or that narrow beam of light which brings the task almost into a world of its own, to the exclusion of just about everything else. This is the narrow beam of light that young racquetball player saw from the tiger emblem on his glove and it is the narrow beam of light you must bring into whatever it is that you are doing.

That first Oakland game after the All-Star break of 1979 tested my theories of building concentration. I was long past the point of a rookie player who wondered what would happen if he didn't throw the ball, but I had suffered many lapses of concentration over the years and knew the work it entailed to get my focus back. Despite all my efforts to plan and strategize the game prior to play, I still fell victim to a loss of concentration. My meditation exercises did not prepare me 100 percent for the distractions on the field. It was at that Oakland game I developed the trick of staring at my glove and my green and brown theory.

I told myself that my performance began on the mound. Once there, nothing else mattered. For the time that I prepared to throw, threw, and followed through, I was required to do nothing else. It was almost like a cocoon built around me. At that moment, I had no other purpose in life. Because I would not allow any other thought to distract me on the mound, I had to find myself an out if distractions occurred. I told myself that on the grass I can think about anything. I can think about paying my bills or wonder what I'm going to have for dinner that night. I can be mad at Earl. If a fan distracted me, I would watch until the commotion settled down. My mind could wander wherever it would.

Obviously I couldn't spend a great deal of time off the mound, either. I needed to develop a trigger to bring my thoughts back on track. I needed a trick to focus. That's when I came up with the idea of staring at the emblem on my glove. I made a rule for myself. Once I started that process, I had to push every other thought away. All emotion on the green; all business on the brown of the mound.

The first time I tried it, I stared at the Wilson "W." I had to force myself to envision it almost coming alive, building light around the edges. I imagined this light concentrating itself into a narrow beam. This was a conscious visualization and it's a good thing the rest of the people in the stadium couldn't read my thoughts. I waited until I was ready, until I saw that beam of light. Then I went up to the mound.

Once there, I was ready. There were no random thoughts, no gazing around the stadium. When I got up on the mound, I knew what I was going to do. I knew how it was going to feel. I could see the ball fly through the air. I was sure of my performance. Preparation. Execution. Success.

Preparation. Execution. Success. One. Two. Three.

This sounds easy, but it isn't. Don't mistake my trick with the emblem on my glove as preparation. It was a part of getting ready to perform, a big part, but

♦

105

there was much that went before it. And being properly prepared is the basis of any success.

There are two kinds of preparation, mental and physical. Up to now, we've been discussing the mental preparation with respect to the emotional barriers to achieving your goals. There is a requirement, however, before any steps can be taken toward any goal. That requirement is energy, both physical and mental.

President John F. Kennedy said, "Physical fitness is the basis for all other forms of excellence." That was back in the 1960s. With today's stress on healthful living, you'd have to live in a cave to not know that eating right, exercise, and doing away with certain habits add to the quality of life. Sometimes, though, when we hear so much about a certain thing, its importance loses its meaning. Does the oat bran question confuse you or don't you even care anymore?

With that in mind, I'm going to add one more voice to the importance of taking care of yourself. To achieve anything, you must have the energy to take and sustain the action which moves you toward your goal. Depending upon your age and basic condition to start with, accumulating this energy can be difficult. There was a point in my life when I could stay up all night, go home and shower, then put in a full day. Let me tell you, that point is long gone. Once I could trade a proper breakfast for a coke and some cold pizza, rush out my front door, and not eat again until I picked up a hamburger around three in the afternoon. In those days, I never had to slow down. Since none of us are teen-agers forever, behavior of this kind not only prevents us from achievement as we get older, it actually retards our ability to move forward.

I'm not suggesting you start weight training in mid-life, although that is certainly achievable if that's what you want to do. What I am saying is that exercise, proper diet, and a healthy lifestyle are requirements to succeed.

♦

Exercise. No, it's not jogging clothes, major muscle groups, and sweat. Exercise can be as simple and inexpensive as a walk every day. As a matter of fact, walking is the best way to start building toward a disciplined, goal-oriented lifestyle. The critical part of an exercise program is that it be sustained.

Exercise is a wonderful thing. In the long run, it adds to your life, both the term and the quality. In the short run, it provides energy. The aerobic nature of walking improves your body's ability to take in and use oxygen. It makes your body function more efficiently, using food as fuel and burning off the excess. As a matter of fact, it will relax you as much as if you'd simply sat down and rested. You will feel better and when you feel better, you will perform better. You will sleep more restfully. You will think more clearly. Studies have shown that as we age past fifty-five, exercise keeps us mentally alert by boosting the circulation system. There are benefits on every level.

Ray Miller, my pitching coach while I was with the Orioles, insisted all pitchers run together at the ballpark. You played as a team, you pitched as a team, so you ran as a team. It was this team concept that had proven so successful for the Orioles organization. I accepted that, but preferred distance running. So at Key Biscayne that year, I ran six miles before practice in the morning and six miles each evening before dinner. This was not so much for the conditioning as for the mental toughness. Let's face it, running six miles hurts. What I was trying to do was condition myself to run through the pain. I felt if I could run these six miles, through all the aches and pains, I could condition myself to pitch into the late innings when my arm started to hurt, when my shoulder began to ache. It was a question of mind over body. And it worked. During that year I completed nine games, about 25 percent of my starts. Even today that is a pretty good average. Of my starts, I averaged about seven innings. So the effort paid off.

As far as Ray Miller's ideas of team effort, they have proved true over time. As the pitching coach for Pittsburgh, Ray helped lead the Pirates to the division title in 1990. Jim Leyland, manager of the Pirates, would be the first to admit that Ray and his style of team coaching had a lot to do with that success.

The same principle will work for you. That first long, brisk walk will tell on aching calves, but go that extra block or two. Push yourself. Build up that mental toughness. It will pay off in added reserves to do late nights at the office, if that is necessary, or one more bucket of practice balls on the driving range, or an extra hour of study.

Once you start exercising, even if it is only a walk every day, you will find yourself looking for other ways to improve how you live. That bag of potato chips you used to eat when you watched television at night won't seem so appetizing any more. The twelve ounce ribeye you used to look forward to will become a rock in your stomach just thinking about it. Seems unbelievable, but it's true. Your body knows what's good for it, even if your mind doesn't. It will tell you what feels right. All you have to do is give it a chance to speak.

After you've begun to exercise and eat right, you will find yourself drifting away from those things that make you feel slow or drained or stressed. You'll begin to notice how bad cigarette smoking makes you feel. No, I'm not going to give you a lecture, I smoke cigars. Start improving your life and your body will do that for you. You won't come home from work and plop yourself in front of the television. You'll have too much energy for that. You'll find yourself looking for things to do. The garage will get cleaned up and the back bedroom painted. And this drive will carry over to your job. Then watch out.

♦

Even your attitude will change. You'll be in a much better frame of mind. Being negative takes more energy than being positive, and negative energy is a waste. You won't deal with that any longer. When you feel better about yourself, you feel better about the people around you. It's a circle. Once you become easier to deal with, they'll become easier to deal with.

Do I sound like some sort of storyteller? Okay, I admit it, but all of this is true. Take a look at those around you who live healthy lives. They are more energetic; they seem to succeed at just about everything the do. Sometimes they tend to be a bit uppity about it, thank you, but they mean no harm. That would take time and energy away from where they want to go.

Don't think that all of this "healthy stuff" is a bunch of hard work, either. It snowballs. The biggest effort is the start, after that, your own desire to feel good will keep the ball rolling. Start today. Take a walk. Bring someone along with you. Nobody said you couldn't have a good time. As a matter of fact, a good time is often its own reward.

In 1983, I was involved with the first ever baseball "fantasy camp." Beloved Cub-great Charlie Grimm, Randy Hundley, and I put together a cross section of businessmen, some from the Chicago Board of Trade, attorneys, doctors, including a psychiatrist, for a spring training in Scottsdale, Arizona. Their goal was to play the 1969 Chicago Cub team. Although many people have copied this idea, and Randy himself has developed the program into a successful business, at the time this was a unique situation. We were covered by the major networks and *Time* magazine. All of us were excited and ready for just about anything.

Randy, catcher for the 1969 Cubs team, was in charge of getting the Cubs into shape. Mine and Charlie's job was to work with the others, the team we wound up calling the "Misfits." We had one week to give these guys a taste of spring training as it really is. We had to get them into shape and motivate them. Although most of them were highly competitive in their own fields, we had to show them how to channel that competitiveness into a successful performance with respect to an athletic endeavor. We saw the same enthusiasm to don a major league uniform that we ourselves, as players, had shown. These were guys just like ourselves, who as kids went to sleep with a mitt and a ball and dreamed of their baseball heroes. It wasn't hard to motivate them.

The first day they were magnificent on the field. Here were these doctors, and lawyers, and captains of industry, all dressed in Chicago Cubs uniforms. We hit them ground balls and fly balls. We worked on cutoffs. They took batting practice. Except for one fellow, whose spring training lasted only four minutes, until he chased after a ball, tore up his knee, and had to spend the rest of the week in the hospital, by the end of the first day my team was tired, but undaunted.

The second day, they seemed to have aged. The enthusiasm may still have been there, but the physical demands were taking their toll. Some of these guys were using muscles they forget they had.

The third day came and it was a lesson in mind over body. We had an exercise instructor, a young lady who came every day to try to ease the pain by helping get the team into shape. Some on the team were hard pressed to believe she made the situation better.

The Cubs players themselves helped out. Players like Ron Santo, Glenn Beckert, Ernie Banks, Don Kessinger, Gene Oliver, and Fergie Jenkins went out of their way to make it easier. I think they got a secondhand thrill being around these guys who were finally getting a chance to play the closest thing to major league ball they'd ever experience.

♦

On the day we finally played our game, I was in the locker room trying to bring my charges to a fevered pitch. Despite sore muscles, it was an easy task. Just as we had taped every practice so these fellows could have a record of their performance, we planned to tape the final game. Also, there was plenty of media around to pick up the story. Not only were they playing major league ball, they were playing to a national audience. Everybody involved wanted these guys to look their best. I reminded them they were playing a lot of older guys. They had had six days of intense training. I told them they had a chance, that they were ready. I was the manager to beat all managers. They had achieved their dream. They were going to be on the field with guys they had only read about, or seen from the stands or on television. This was their moment. I had my guys ready. They were worked up into a frenzy. They were ready to run through walls. They were as psychologically ready as they could possibly be.

Fergie Jenkins, winner of twenty or more games from 1967 to 1972, started the game for the Cubs. I don't think I could have done anything different to prepare my team to play. But, in the end, the "Misfits" were slaughtered by the 1969 Cubs, the final score being something like twenty-five to six. But, for all of those guys who had actually made a major leaguer miss a pitch or even strike out, for every time one of the "Misfits" made a successful play, the entire effort was worth it.

This might have been the 1969 Cubs team playing in 1983, but the physical skills possessed by professional athletes don't fade overnight. On the other hand, not even months of preparation could bring a group of professional businessmen, attorneys, and doctors to the level of a major league player, albeit one past his prime. Here was a group of people taking a risk on achieving a goal. The risk was the achieve-

◆

ment of a dream. I hope that for a few moments before the game, these guys thought they could actually win. If so, I did my job. I don't think, though, that in the clear light of day, any of them actually *believed* they would win. Was it, then, a programmed failure because there was no real chance to succeed? I don't think so. Was the experience a successful one for my "Misfits"? You bet.

The second aspect of preparation is mental. Before you start any task, you must know the proper technique for accomplishing it. If your goal is to be a doctor, go to school. If you aspire to be a musician, education and practice are the foundation. The top salesperson, knowledge of your product and market.

During my meditations, I pitched the game. I visualized every batter, imagined his strengths and weaknesses, made a mental game of pitching against every possible situation. I knew what I was going to do in any situation. This is the basis of mental preparation, the analysis of the task and the development of responses to the progress of this task.

After knowledge, comes concentration. This is a skill which can be learned and there are master teachers. Andy Messersmith who played for both the Angels and the Dodgers, for example. You could look at his eyes on the mound and see how well he was able to concentrate. He is a great example of a pitcher willing the ball into the catcher's glove. He was so focused with his eyes that it did not matter what pitch he intended to throw or where the glove was, he was undaunted. Tom Seaver was another one. His whole physical demeanor was one of complete control. Again, the truth was in his eyes. Total commitment. And there are others.

For every one of those who exhibit this skill, there are others who are perfect examples of what happens when we lose concentration. Steve Trout, for example. A physically gifted player but prone to lapses in

♦

112

concentration. I would be broadcasting from the booth and watch Trout mow down player after player for five straight innings. The guy never let up. Then he'd lose it. Little things gave him away. He'd begin to take more time on the mound. His facial expression changed. The look in his eyes was gone. There is almost a glow in the eye when concentration and intensity are there. I could tell by looking at Steve that he'd lost concentration. The same is true for all of us.

I had to work at concentration. In time, the exercises became so entrenched in my behavior, it took no time at all to visualize that narrow beam of light, refocus and get on with the task. I don't know if Andy or Tom ever had to work to achieve this focus. Perhaps they had the natural ability to turn their attention completely away from distraction and to the task at hand. If they did, that was one less stumbling block for them to overcome. If they didn't, one has to applaud the success with which they moved on toward their goal.

Losing concentration in the workplace is just as damaging as losing it on the field. For me, now, it's more embarrassing, too. Being a color man for the Cubs on WGN, if I lose concentration, I make a mistake.

A color man waits for the play-by-play man, who in my case is Harry Caray, to stop before he comes in. For three to three and a half hours each broadcast, my attention has to be totally on the game. One little distraction and I could miss a player switch, a fly ball to left field, or even a home run.

My job in the booth is to anticipate the action, and when my concentration is strong, it's almost like predicting the future. It has to be. Without those few moments to gather my thoughts, I couldn't be sure of relevant comment.

Actually, anticipating what is going to happen is a bit more scientific than looking into a crystal ball.

♦

After watching the players over a period of time, I have learned what to look for in their behavior. I find myself to be a much more talented observer in the booth than I ever was in the dugout. For one thing I can see more. I have learned to key in on certain players. I know how a runner's hands move at first base to tell what he's going to do next. Sometimes, when a player's ready to steal, he moves differently than on the previous four pitches. I'll say to the viewer, "I think he'll go on the next pitch." I'm guessing, I'm not a prophet. But I've gotten better at guessing.

Broadcasting sports requires intense concentration. It's live television at its most challenging. When you're on mike, you have to be ready for anything. When I first started out, I thought the most difficult situations would arise from the field. I learned otherwise in 1982, quite early in my tenure on ABC's "Monday Night Baseball," with Howard Cosell.

I was telling a story about Joe Torre at one of our production meetings for "Monday Night Baseball." Joe, now the manager for the St. Louis Cardinals, was a wonderful player with the Braves, the Cardinals and the Mets, who I had known since 1971 when I was with the Giants. That was the year Joe hit .363, which, for a man who couldn't run a lick, was quite an accomplishment. When I was with the Cubs, Joe was playing for the Mets and manager Joe Frazier. We were in the outfield before a game discussing Frazier's use of Joe. "This guy's not playing me against right-handed pitchers. (Joe was a right-handed hitter.) I've got over 2,500 hits, most of them against right-handed pitchers. I can't believe he's platooning me."

I was telling this story because Boston, which was one of the scheduled teams, had been platooning two of their outfielders, Rick Miller and Reid Nichols. I wanted to illustrate that at times platooning was not the best strategic move, sometimes the wrong players were platooned or young players were platooned before a true evaluation could be made of their batting skills. I said Joe Torre was a guy who'd be a hitter for years, he could hit anybody, no problem. All during this meeting, Howard sat listening.

During the seventh inning, a pitching change was made and, right on cue, Boston flip-flopped Nichols for Miller. That sent the booth into a discussion of the platoon system. Then Howard came in.

"Reminds me of the time that the aging Joe Torre, playing for the New York Mets under then manager Joe Frazier, was bemoaning the fact that he was being platooned. And he had over 2,500 hits. And he said to Joe Frazier, 'I can't believe you're platooning me.' You see how crazy it gets platooning players who quite obviously have All-Star talent." And Howard went on. And on. And on.

When he was finished he turned to me and said, "Comments, Steve?"

Concentration was not the only thing I lost that day.

After preparation, comes the execution. You've heard the commercial—"Just Do It." If you're properly prepared, execution follows quite easily.

There is a rhythm, both mental and physical, to every activity and nothing can impart this rhythm except practice. Those of you who play golf know exactly what I'm talking about. Timing is everything. Coupled with concentration, it is unbeatable. Just look at Jack Nicklaus. Here is a man who can almost will the flight of the ball in the air. Imagine the amount of concentration it took for Jack to win that last Masters. The picture of him coming down "Amen Corner" at Augusta National knowing that he'd won, that late in his career, is a lesson to everyone, not just professional athletes. Jack set his mind to the task and performed.

Each activity has its own physical groove, even if that activity is more mental than physical. By physi-

◆

115

cal groove, I don't just mean the muscle movement required to perform the task, I also mean the whole process by which the task is accomplished. The pattern of performance.

The days on which I played, I got up each morning and followed the same routine, breakfast, a walk, a little reading, then meditation. Every day on which I played, the same thing. There was a timing to these activities that had nothing to do with a clock. Each element of my day was meant to provide input to my task and get myself ready. As you approach each day, with a short-range, mid-range, and long-range goal in mind, the same thing is required of you. You must set up your physical and mental pattern to make the accomplishment of this goal the natural result of your behavior to that point.

How many of you truly plan your day? I'm not talking about getting up in the morning and saying to yourself, I've got to finish this report by four o'clock. I'm talking about a detailed plan for your day with every step focused on the achievement of a goal. With training, this detailed plan can become a natural result of your daily routine. Much like a golfer swings to the tempo of his own body's rhythm, you will think clearly and efficiently if you create a mental groove for yourself.

For me, the most effective way to start creating this mental groove was to keep lists. I had to get up each morning and write down what I had to, or wanted to, accomplish that day. I did this before I showered or even had a first cup of coffee. Then I prioritized my list, nothing new or magic about it. After determining what I had to do and the order in which I wanted to do it, I assigned a time limit to each activity. Very early on I learned there was never enough hours in the day, and I underestimated the time on just about everything. The last thing I did each night was review the list.

♦

What I learned about myself was amazing. First, I learned how much time I wasted both in doing activities which were not important and in letting outside influences steer me away from what I wanted to do. Letting my answering machine screen my phone calls now is a major time saver.

Second, I was made aware of those things that consumed most of my time. Knowing this made me focus on the question of evaluating what I was doing with my life.

Lastly, seeing my schedule in writing enabled me to plan more effectively, coordinating activities and combining effort.

A pattern evolved. During my days as a player with the Orioles, my goal was to become the best pitcher I could be. Anything on my daily list which interfered with that goal had to be eliminated, or at least minimized. You can do the same thing.

Given time, you won't have to write down your daily schedule. This detailed planning process will become part of your morning routine. And that's all a physical or mental groove is, a routine. The trick is to make this routine productive and goal-oriented. Just like with a golf swing, or how a mechanic uses his tools, or how a musician handles his instrument, it is rhythm. If the rhythm is sound, the performance will be successful.

Be aware, though, that this concentration and rhythm is easily broken. During that 1980 season, when I had perfected the method of visualization, planning, and concentration, I was still vulnerable to outside influence.

We were playing the Cleveland Indians at Memorial Stadium. I was rolling along in the seventh inning with a two to nothing lead. Cleveland didn't have a particularly powerful team and we had pretty good success against them. The only player to hit more than eleven home runs for them was rookie Joe

◆

Charboneau, who ended up winning the Rookie of the Year.

With two outs in the seventh and a man on first, I worked the count on Charboneau to no balls and two strikes. My irrepressible catcher, Rick Dempsey, a wonderful man who is now trying to make the 1991 Milwaukee Brewer team after spending time with the Los Angeles Dodgers, calls a time-out and strolls to the mound. Dempsey says to me, "Look, this is the only guy in the lineup who can hit a home run off you. So whatever you do, don't hang a curveball."

Now it had not occurred to me that I would hang a curveball. I had been rolling right along. I said, "Well, thanks." My rhythm and concentration had been broken.

Rick went back and flashed two fingers signaling for a curveball. I promptly hung a curveball. Almost as if it were a movie script, Joe Charboneau hit a home run to tie it up at two to two. I did not beat the Cleveland Indians that day.

I told Rick Dempsey later on, "Never come to the mound again if you don't have anything better to say than that. It never occurred to me to hang a curveball until you came out and mentioned something about it. If you're going to go to the mound, always speak positively. Don't say what *not* to do. The pitcher is perfectly aware of what *not* to do. Say what *to* do. You should have told me to strike him out."

Now that you've got the energy and the concentration necessary to succeed, your goals set, and your life cleared of unnecessary clutter, you're ready to decide whether you can handle success.

And you thought the hard part was over.

Do You Really Want to Be a Winner?

Will you do *anything* to win?

A heady question if I ever heard one, but one which also gets right to the point of what exactly it is you want.

Now that you've got the tools you need to be successful, you have to decide if that's the road you really want to take. Up to now, all we've discussed is the methods by which success can be achieved, the erasure of negative belief systems, the ability to visualize success, the skill of concentration. These are important. What we haven't talked about is the desire to be successful.

Let's take a look at someone who has been overweight all his life. If that person does not feel good

♦

about himself, his behavior shows it. He will tend to be withdrawn when put in new situations. He will act in the manner others expect him to rather than the way he would have chosen for himself. He will be reluctant to take risks. He will not look upon himself as a winner.

This person then successfully loses weight. What should happen at that point is that his behavior changes. He should be more relaxed in a crowd, more honest in his reactions, more likely to experiment with unfamiliar situations. He should have a more aggressive image of himself. Many times, though, that just doesn't happen.

Instead of using an overweight person as an example, we can use someone who undergoes cosmetic surgery, someone who goes back for that college degree after many years away from school, even someone who finally wins the lottery after years of buying tickets. Pick any person in any situation where they achieve something they think they want. How often do things really stay the same for that person? More often than we think.

The reason for this is fear of success, or more accurately, fear of change. Change is a threatening part of our lives, and, along with death, the most inevitable. When we decide that we are going to take control of our lives and manage our own success, we are not only going to experience change, we are going to invite it into our lives. Therefore, we must be ready for the stress change brings with it.

Take a look at your list of goals. Every one of these has a price tag over and above the kinds of efforts we've been talking about.

You want a more challenging job. You've changed your behavior at work and the bosses have noticed. You used to be someone who didn't question what he was told to do, now you demand to know the whys and whos of your job. You make sure you understand the purpose behind the task. In the process of this, you've

♦

come up with a few good suggestions which have been implemented. You've gone from an employee who performs satisfactorily to one who excels. Finally, you've got what you wanted. You're the boss. You have the money. You have the prestige. You have the power. And you've got the headaches. Did you think about that part when you put "better job" on your list?

Bear in mind, the more successful you are, the harder you are going to work. You're going to need all that energy you've been building. You may have started with a job you could forget about when you were not there, but the higher one rises in the organization, the less time away from the job there is, on the clock or off. The challenges are greater, more complex, and the responsibility to meet these challenges cannot be turned off at five o'clock.

These new demands and the changes they bring will not just affect you on the job; they will carry over into the rest of your life. There may be a game or two that you will miss even though your child is in the starting lineup. You might have less time to spend working on that project in the garage. You may not keep up with your favorite television show any longer.

The changes in your life may be even more subtle, but no less threatening. These walks you've been taking every night are showing in your energy level, your attitude, and your improved conditioning. Your family could resent this. Sounds strange but it's true. Of course, they want good things for you, but the changes you are undergoing are changes for them, too. Since your family has not invited these changes themselves, the threat appears even more ominous. Perhaps they don't understand your sudden interest in your job. Over the years they've gotten so used to you complaining about it, this new behavior is something they are unable to comprehend.

One of the most extreme examples of this happened to a couple of friends of mine. This couple had been married for many years. Dan was an alcoholic. Mary suffered through it. I can't count the number of conversations Mary and I had in which she said, "If he'd only stop drinking, everything would be fine." Mary vacillated between concern, frustration, and anger, but mostly anger.

One day, on his own, seemingly out of the blue, Dan checked himself into a rehabilitation clinic. Mary called me. She was angrier than if she had found him facedown on the lawn. It's not that she would have preferred that, but she couldn't understand his sudden change in behavior and resented the threat this change posed to the pattern of living she had so carefully constructed. The stronger Dan became, the angrier Mary was. This is classic codependency. And each one of us develops codependent behavior to our environment, whether that environment is destructive or not.

Are you prepared to face the difficulties your new, positive behavior presents? Communication is the key to overcoming any problems that arise. You've been honest with yourself, now you have to be honest with those around you.

It's time to make a new list. Take out your sheet of goals. Choose one. Evaluate what it is going to cost. These are some of the questions you're going to have to answer:

What is the price of this goal? In terms of time. Money. Sacrifices I will have to make. Sacrifices my family or friends will have to make. Am I willing to pay this price? Are they?

After you've answered these questions, there's more. What do you expect to happen when you reach this goal? Are you sure these end results are what you want? If what you want to be is the boss, are you aware of all that entails? If you learn to play the piano proficiently, what does that mean to you? Will you be satisfied with the knowledge that you have learned, or is it something else you are truly after?

Are you prepared to change your self-image? Are you prepared for others not to change their view of you? What is most important to you?

Challenging questions for sure, but ones which must be addressed at some point because the greater the change you envision for yourself, the more you will change your environment. And that environment may not want to be changed.

Is the achievement of your goal what you hoped it would be?

There's a way to find out before you commit your resources to achievement. Visualize having achieved what you want. In the same way you examined all the possible outcomes of dealing with a problem, examine the possibilities once you've achieved success. Relax and see yourself.

Remember, though, when you see yourself having reached your goal, fill in the background. Take the other important factors in your life, your family, your friends, co-workers, feel the absence of those things you had to give up along the way. Watch yourself as you enjoy having reached your goal. Take note of your expectations.

Do you see an audience on its feet at Carnegie Hall after you've finished that piece on the piano? If you do, simply learning to play will not satisfy you. Reexamine the goal.

If what you want is a high paying job after you've finally earned the college degree, visualizing the graduation ceremony will not be enough. See yourself at a desk, late at night, correcting mistakes. You may be in your own office, but being the boss is more than furniture and a room.

The point here is to look at your goals realistically. Don't think that simple achievement is the same as fulfillment. If you think so, you are in for a major setback.

My goal was to be the best pitcher in the major leagues. From July 1979 through 1980, I was. Those who made sport of the fact that I had a Cy Young Award clause in my contract with the Orioles had to eat their words. In 1980, I was the best. In 1982, I was forced to leave baseball.

During 1982, it got to the point where I felt there was no more baseball left in me. In May, I took two cortisone shots in my elbow one week apart from each other. Then I went out to throw. I couldn't do it like I wanted to. I kept trying. I tried to visualize myself pitching, but something in the process wasn't right. From out of nowhere the thought hit me, "It's time to quit." I was shaken.

On my way to the park that day, I was torn. For eighteen months I convinced myself to meditate, visualize, follow my instincts. The process was successful. Should I follow the process now? For two days, I labored over the question. I wasn't leaving baseball to do something else. I was quitting because I could no longer do myself or the game justice. Finally, I knew what I had to do. I went to Hank Peters, at the time general manager of the Orioles, now general manager of the Cleveland Indians. "I can't help you any more. It's time to look to elsewhere."

Years of injuries had taken their toll on my arm. Sure, I could probably have played a couple of more years, taking cortisone shots, going through rehabilitation therapy, generally watching my arm deteriorate until surgery was the only option. Then would come the excuses for poor performance, this time with a definite basis in fact. The struggle I put myself through in 1979 and 1980 would be looked upon as a fluke by my team, the fans, the writers. In time, I'd come to believe it, too. I had to admit to myself that the quality of my career would never again be what I

♦

wanted it to be. The best pitcher I could possibly be was not good enough any more. I had to face that fact.

Giving up my lifetime ambition of playing professional baseball was the hardest thing I have ever done.

Although I left the field financially secure, my restaurants were doing well, I worked steadily as a color commentator on television, the first five years after my retirement were hell. I would dream constantly of a comeback. At night, I could see myself throwing in spring training. I pitched and I still had the stuff. My subconscious seemed not to want to let go.

In my dreams, I was back in the limelight. The memory is a wonderful tool. It tends to heighten the good times and dissolve the bad. The longer you're away from something, the better the experience seems. The bad times fade away into this gray mist where those experiences lose definition; the good times sparkle in the sunlight. For years after my retirement, in my dreams I could play again.

In the light of day, I was a bit more practical. Coaches would invite me to throw batting practice. I always refused. I was afraid, not of doing poorly, but of doing well. What a temptation to go back to the game. For me, it was time to quit and get on with my life. For others, the decision is not necessarily the same.

I sat next to Tommy John a couple of years ago at a roast for Harry Caray. Tommy was then in his mid-forties, one of the oldest players in the major leagues. He said to me "I'd like to play another year. I still think I can do it."

The man had played twenty-nine years of professional baseball. Was it time to take off the uniform? Not for Tommy John because he still believed he could do it. At the time I thought maybe he can. He's healthy. Very few players ever leave the major leagues healthy. Tommy had suffered some tremendous injuries early on, forcing a tendon transplant from his leg to his elbow, but in later years he had not had the

♦

type of injuries that force others to leave the sport. Would there be another spring training in the life of Tommy John? He felt the Yankees were wrong in letting him go. Since that time Tommy has retired. If the decision were totally his, perhaps he wouldn't have.

Trying to come back is a trap. You see it in boxers, Joe Frazier, Muhammad Ali, George Foreman. In tennis players like John McEnroe. Rumor has it that Bjorn Borg is even thinking of coming back. These guys won't give up the ghost. Perhaps some level of physical skill is still there. In John McEnroe's case this was evident in the 1990 U.S. Open, but physical skill is not the only requirement to be a winner. We know that. It takes a deep and concentrated mental and emotional commitment. To win you need it all. Coming back for the money or because of the fame will not cut it. There comes a point when you have to divorce yourself from one aspect of your life, let it go, so you can do justice to the rest of your life. If you don't, you fail not just once but twice.

There is a poem by Alfred Houseman, "To An Athlete Dying Young." In it a young man dies right after his greatest triumph. He is remembered with respect and awe. The poet thinks this is a wonderful thing, because with his death, the athlete has insured he will always be thought of in greatness. He will never suffer the humiliation of trying to achieve the pinnacle of success again only to experience defeat.

It is the same with all of us. We must know when, what once was a goal, becomes fantasy. For me, listening to what my subconscious was telling me that day in 1982 was the best decision of my life.

The call from ABC's "Monday Night Baseball" came as I gave my retirement speech. The morning after, David Hartman called me to see if I could be on "Good Morning America." After the show he asked if I had time for breakfast. "I have the rest of my life," I told him.

◆

"Your timing is excellent," David said, referring to my offer from ABC. "It couldn't have been more perfect. There's two guys in baseball right now who can pull it off on television, Jim Palmer and Tom Seaver. If you retired when they retire, they would get the TV jobs. But they're still playing and by the time they stop you will have as much experience in the business as you need. You'll be able to go anywhere."

Truly listening to myself set up the rest of my life. It is the key to knowing what to do. Too many people listen to words and not feelings. They choose to hear what they want to hear and not the truth. All of us have an intuitive sense about what is right for us in any situation. Don't romanticize the issue and be captivated by what's on the surface. Dig deep. You don't have to live with past failures and you don't have to hold on to old dreams.

The same honesty can be applied to the evaluation of achievement. There is a wide gap between satisfaction in performance and the achievement of goals. Back to my original goal of being the best pitcher in the major leagues.

As I applied the techniques in this book, my level of performance improved. Remember, the goal was to be the best pitcher in the majors, not to go 25–7, not to win the Cy Young Award, not to get a bigger contract. With that, as I began to rack up wins, I could have quite easily let the pride and satisfaction of improved performance be enough. Or become more than satisfied as I watched my record steadily and quite rapidly improve. I didn't.

Part of the reason for this is the nature of competitive sports. There is no room for slacking off in determination. Earl Weaver's threat to put me in the bullpen and not start me reminded me of that. However, in many other phases of life, the opportunity to relax once a level of achievement is reached presents itself.

♦

Take the goal of getting a better job. Once you have been promoted, once the congratulations have been passed out, once you have been accustomed to living on your higher income, there are many opportunities to relax, to let your performance slide into the same habits as before. After all, you got what you wanted.

The problem with satisfaction is that it breeds complacency. John Teets said it best, "Contentment can kill a career."

Moments of satisfaction occur, to be sure, but if you get to the point where you're satisfied with everything, you might as well pack it in. We are always evolving. These times when we have reached a level in our life where we can look back and say, "In this, I'm the best that I can be" allow us to appreciate what we have, keep our sanity. We all know, though, that life moves to quickly to allow us to do that for long. It's like the log rollers who can never stop. They never really control that log. They can't step back and say, "What a beautiful day," they'd be swallowed up. They can slow the log down, but they can never stop. Like them, we must continue to move forward.

If you think I'm suggesting you spend the rest of your life dissatisfied with what you have, I'm not. Goal setting is a positive thing. In looking at the present, you should be able to say, "Yes, this is good. I have done well." To the future, you must add, "But this can be better."

There is no rule that says a goal cannot change. Mine had to when I could no longer perform to a standard required of my job. Physical limitations are not the only reasons to redirect your goals, though. Circumstances change. You get married, divorced. The company you work for goes out of business. You win the lottery. You simply decide that you no longer want what you once thought you did. Believe me, "I don't want this any more" is one of the most valid reasons to change direction. Self-analysis is an ongo-

◆

ing process. The desire to accomplish just one more thing is the greatest motivator.

My father is my biggest supporter and my most astute critic. I have depended upon his wisdom for as long as I can remember. He and my mother had one of the most rewarding relationships I have ever witnessed. They functioned as one without losing their individuality. They were each other's strength. Theirs was everything a marriage should be.

When my mother died, my own sense of loss became overshadowed by concern for my father. He had his health, he had friends, and he still had my sister and I for emotional support. Despite all that, my mother's passing was a devastating loss. He might well have decided to give up. Reactions like that are not uncommon, and in traumatic situations we tend to think of ourselves in one dimensional terms. My father could have concentrated on himself as a husband and become overwhelmed by grief for his wife. But he was also a friend, and a parent. I did not want to lose him.

"Are you planning to join her," I blurted out, suddenly sorry I asked, but wanting desperately to know.

My father looked me straight in the eye. "No. I still have some things to do."

When he said that, I knew, in time, he would be all right.

Keeping in mind that we are all going to die, you might as well go for as many of the triumphs as you can, big triumphs, little triumphs, major goals, secondary goals. On a day-to-day basis, it's this sense of achievement that keeps us motivated. One win gives you the incentive to go for another.

Having a clear picture of what you truly want enables you to more effectively achieve it. Getting what you want is the best thing that can happen.

♦

Changing Goals

When I walked out of the interview room after having given my retirement speech, the secretary for the Orioles handed me two telephone messages. David Hartman wanted me on "Good Morning America" for the second time, and Chuck Howard, vice-president for ABC Sports wanted me to call him. "I think he has a job for you," Helen Conklin said. "You better give him a call."

I was not leaving baseball to do anything else, and I was fully aware that sixty days from my retirement it would be "Steve who?" I did not feel the need to take any time off. I was unemployed. TV work appealed to me. I took the message from Helen's hand. "Right away."

After the great year I had in 1980, I was on "The Today Show," and "Good Morning America," on the cover of several sports magazines, and in *People* magazine. I did a couple of endorsements. I was interviewed frequently on sportscasts. With all this going on, I was not surprised when I got call from the Epilepsy Foundation. They wanted me to do a telethon in Baltimore. I was down at spring training, but I flew back from camp to do it. How much could this take?

When I got to the studio, I figured I'd be there ten minutes. Say hi to the fans. Talk a little baseball. Meet some folks. Ask for money. Get on a plane and go back to Florida. Piece of cake.

One of the local news anchormen came up to me. "How are you?"

"Fine. Pretty busy around here."

"Sure is."

We're carrying on this conversation as if everything were just fine. Then he turns to me and says, "I think I better fill you in a little bit. The first hour we're going to be doing this, then we're going to show some clips of that, so-and-so will be here for an interview . . ."

I politely listened, waiting for him to get to the point.

"And the second hour, we're going to be doing this. If so-and-so shows up, we're going to do the interview right then. We've got some kids who've collected money in their neighborhoods, we'll bring them in around halfway through."

I wished he'd hurry up. He was sure taking the long way around.

"And in the third hour, we'll start off with . . ."

"Hold it," I said, "just tell me where I come in."

"This is three hours of live coverage." He almost looked surprised.

"That's okay. But where do I come in?"

"That's what I'm telling you. In the first hour . . ."

♦

131

"Wait a minute," I stopped him again. "What are you telling me?

"Why, you and I are co-hosts." He said it as if it were the most natural thing in the world.

"Co-hosts! I've never even interviewed anybody!"

"Don't worry," he said. "You'll love it."

He was right.

So when Chuck Howard of ABC made me an offer, I couldn't refuse. "Keith Jackson is going on vacation. We thought you might be interested in doing a couple of games for us. Interested?"

You bet.

Remembering my previous experience, I knew that I could be relaxed in front of a camera, but let's face it, TV sports broadcasting is a sophisticated business. The anchormen are sharp and there's no room for the caricature of the bumbling athlete. I needed to do well.

My method to insure success was the same. I relaxed and let myself visualize the experience. I told myself that I was going to be bright, articulate, concise. The last thing I ever wanted to be was one of those color men who didn't know when to stop.

I knew something about timing, having watched enough televised games in my lifetime. I knew how the booth system worked. Al Michaels, the play-by-play man, would have the microphone before every pitch. The microphone would then go to Don Drysdale. If I wanted to make a point, I would have to do it after Don was through and before the microphone went back to Al.

I visualized myself making salient points, covering issues that as a player I had just taken for granted, but as a broadcaster I had to present in such a way that those who weren't baseball insiders could understand. "Don't take anything for granted," I was warned before I got into the booth. "Explain as much as you can. Keep it as simple as possible."

♦

I watched myself broadcast the entire game on an imaginary television set. Afterwards, I saw Al Michaels say, "You did a great job. I can't believe it. You were really good. You were educational, informative, funny." By the time I was finished, I was confident of how I would look and was sure of how I would perform. Then I went off to do it, no training, no instruction, just the knowledge that I would succeed.

It went smoothly. At the end of the show, Al Michaels took off his headset and turned to me. "I've been in this business sixteen years and I've never seen a first-timer as comfortable as you with the broadcast. I think you did a terrific job. You seem to be a natural at this. I think you've got a good future in broadcasting." Unlike early in my baseball career when I had built myself up for failure, this time I built myself up for success.

Self-fulfilling prophecies can be positive, too. To be honest, I was fortunate in having good circumstances my first time out. Al and Don were two of the most supportive people I have ever worked with.

The second game I worked with Al Michaels and Howard Cosell. That was a completely different ballgame.

Al took me aside at lunch that day. "We got an entirely different set of circumstances here because you've never worked with Howard. Let me explain to you what you'll be up against because there's a fine line between what you can and can't do.

"Howard is very powerful with the network. So you have three choices. One, you can agree with everything Howard says about this game. If you do that, you will make a very powerful ally in Howard Cosell and you will lose your credibility with every baseball aficionado in the country.

"Two, you can disagree with everything Howard says, maintain your credibility, for whatever that's worth, and you will make a very powerful enemy in Howard.

◆

133

"Or you can broadcast a game within a game, trying to placate Howard while maintaining some journalistic credibility. Try to explain the game as best you can. Pass on what you think you can. Dance between the raindrops."

How could this happen to me on my second game? I opted for option three. At the time it seemed to be the only alternative.

Needless to say, Howard was Howard.

The game pitted the Detroit Tigers versus the Boston Red Sox. Hard-throwing Dan Petry was on the mound for the Tigers, with Lance Parrish behind the plate. The broadcast was going smoothly until Rich Gedman, catcher for the Red Sox, stepped up to face Petry.

With a runner on first and the count no balls and two strikes, Parrish calls for Petry to waste a pitch low and away. Lance sets up about three or four inches outside, and Petry rears back and throws a ninety-five-mile-an-hour fastball high and inside. The ball goes between the batter and Parrish and up to the screen, with the runner at first moving to second.

Al goes into his bit, "Ball goes to the screen . . .," describing the action. I get on and say, "I would hope they wouldn't charge Parrish with a passed ball because he obviously wanted the ball three or four inches outside. Petry, a major league pitcher, threw the ball up and in. He missed his spot by four feet. Now, if Parrish is setting up inside, he's going to be able to catch that ball. But it's close to impossible to move from three or four inches outside to four feet across the plate up and inside and make a play like that when the man throws the ball ninety-five miles an hour. Looks to me like Petry should be charged with a wild pitch."

Howard reared. "Absolutely not! That is a passed ball. A major league catcher has got to be able to make that play. No doubt about it, it's a passed ball."

♦

No sooner did the words get out of Howard's mouth, then the official scorer ruled. "Wild pitch."

Instead of letting it go, Howard took up the cause. "I cannot believe the official scorekeeper. Who is that man? Thoroughly incompetent call."

I certainly hadn't visualized that scenario before the game.

Chuck Howard's original thought had been for me to cover only two games. That was his offer in the original phone call; but, before I had even begun announcing for ABC, he changed his mind. "We don't think it's fair to evaluate you on two games. We could get you a third, but it means you leave right away for four days in Montreal. I know you haven't been in the National League since 1976. Would you feel comfortable doing that?"

"Chuck, I'd do Japanese baseball, just put me on the air."

Maybe the knowledge that I was going to get at least one more game got me through the Howard Cosell-wild pitch fiasco. Whatever the case, I was fortunate to be back with the Michaels-Drysdale team.

Before each game as a broadcaster, I would work on my concentration and review stats that I was not familiar with. This was live broadcasting. There were no trial runs, no tape recorders on the top of the stands. A lot of football broadcasters will sit in a booth next to the television booth and mock broadcast a game. Here, we didn't do that. My first broadcast had been only four days after my retirement from baseball and already I was comfortable with my new goal. Why? Because I was prepared mentally and emotionally to face the new task.

There's a game I play when I begin to contemplate a new direction. Before I see myself actually performing my new task, I visualize preparing for it. I shower, shave, and dress. I not only visualize my physical performance, I visualize my whole demeanor. I control the image I project. Image may not be everything, but it's a good part of winning.

Breaking each new activity down into its smallest components can assist in understanding what is required of the task, thereby facilitating its completion. Believe me, when you look at winning a baseball game as a whole, it is a very difficult task, almost a monumental one depending upon the team you're facing.

One of the first "Monday Night Baseball" games I was involved in as a player was against the Milwaukee Brewers, and at the time they had some tough hitters. I thought the best way to plan my performance was not to conceive of the game as a whole but to string together a series of pitches. Paul Molitor, one of their best hitters, was up first. What I had to do was envision that first strike and get that behind me. Then I went to the second strike. Pitch by pitch, I struck Molitor out. Then I had to get Robin Yount out. Then Cecil Cooper and Gorman Thomas. I couldn't even think about pitching an inning at a time or even a batter at a time. What I thought about was each individual pitch.

Over time, I became very adept at harnessing the mental processes, going through my mental gymnastics, to accomplish the goal. These gymnastics, if you will, allowed me to break down each game into its simplest parts. An average baseball game is 135 pitches. If you think of it as a whole, the task is overwhelming. I thought of it as a series of pitches, one by one, and the performance was successful. In the Milwaukee game, I gave up a home run to Charlie Moore in the third, and then I retired every hitter until I walked Don Money in the ninth. Tippy Martinez finished out the game for me, and we won two to one.

If you want to break 100 on the golf course, you must first work on your strokes. Your drive, fairway woods, irons, chipping and putting. Each one of these has its own steps, the stance, the shifting of weight, the grip, the follow-through. By breaking each goal into its smallest component, you set yourself up for a series of smaller successes and make the larger goal much more achievable.

Something else I have found a great help over the years is a journal. No, not a diary, a journal. The difference is that a diary records your life in sequence, focusing on the events of the day. A journal records your feelings, your thoughts, your outlook. Journals encourage comment and evaluation. Not only does writing a journal help me crystalize my thoughts, but I often find it helpful to read what I have written before, to remind me of reasons I may have forgotten and to help me review my progress.

Journal keeping does not require a great deal of time, nor great literary skill. The book is yours; it is private. Forget your writing skills, go for the meaning. Five or ten minutes a day is all it really takes.

Have you ever watched a tennis match and seen the players pump themselves up. They talk to themselves, make a fist, yell even. Basically, what they're doing is giving themselves a pep talk. I do it all the time. Sometimes, even aloud. It's being your own coach. And why not? There's no one better.

Analyze past performance. Forget about all the negative inputs you've built in your mind. Take a hard look. Why was this particular incident successful? Why did it fail? If it failed, what do you have to do differently the next time so it will be successful? If it was successful, can you repeat the performance?

Demand excellence. Constant vigilance is needed to monitor behavior and keep it on track.

Pete Rose said one of the reasons he was able to break Ty Cobb's career hit record is that he never had a wasted at-bat. If he was four for four, he never considered that the next time at-bat wouldn't be successful. The rest of us would consider four for five

◆

137

a great day. The fifth time he was able to bear down and get that fifth hit, just like it was his first. This mental toughness allowed him to become the all-time hit leader in the major leagues.

A 75 percent success record separates the winners from the losers. And the winners are not satisfied at that level. Consistent quality performance requires continuous mental preparation. You have to be able to alter your method if circumstances change. You must be alert to change. Some days the fastball is just not there. Some pitchers still try to play it anyway. Winning pitchers recognize that there are days when their physical skills are just not there. They have to be smarter than the guys they are playing against. He has to be able to say to himself, "This batter sees me as a ninety-five mile an hour fastball pitcher. Just wait until he sees my curve."

When Dennis Martinez was at his best, he could beat anybody. For the longest time, though, he was about a .500 pitcher. On those days when he didn't have it all, he wasn't as good. He was a one-way performer. Now Martinez is having one of the best periods in his career. He's gotten older. He's also gotten smarter. With the Montreal Expos, he has three-quarters of the physical tools he had when we played together with the Orioles. But he's finally discovered the secret to the game. Adjustment. Just like Rick Sutcliffe, Dennis has found his method of achievement.

I realize all these things I've been telling you to do may seem silly. At first, they will be uncomfortable because you probably are not used to focusing in on yourself in this manner.

When we first discussed meditation, did you balk? Not for me, you said. Not until you realized you were probably doing it anyway. The only difference between what you've been doing all along and what I'm asking you to do now is structure.

♦

What about all those lists? Something you didn't do unless you were going to the store? Nobody can remember everything. There's no reason not to write it down. So you feel ill at ease with paper and pencil. So what? Who's going to look at these lists anyway? They're not for publication; they're to help you focus on where you want to go, how you want to get there, and what is stopping you from doing it.

What about this visualization stuff? Nothing but daydreams, you say. In some ways that's true, but combined with meditation techniques they can clarify your goals. If you can see yourself in a situation, set up circumstances, and play with alternatives, you will be better prepared to handle all those curves life throws you.

Think you're too far gone to get back in shape. No one is that far gone. There is always something you can do to improve. I've seen elderly people turn themselves around. Even with crippling illnesses, they manage to get on with their lives productively and with purpose.

Too busy to learn to concentrate? That's like saying you're too busy to pay attention. When you force yourself to take a fresh look at those things which have become too familiar, certainly you will be spending more time doing whatever it is that you're doing. That added time will improve your results.

Don't be afraid to write down what you think. For less than a dollar, you can get loose leaf paper and a pencil. Sit down at the kitchen table. Write down what you think—about anything. There are no irrelevant thoughts and no unimportant subjects. If you are in doubt about something, discuss it with yourself. Perhaps by doing that, you will find the answer.

Be your own coach. Demand that extra effort from yourself. Remind yourself of the things you need to do. Reinforce those things you do right. Talk your way through those things that give you a problem.

♦

Give yourself a pep talk whenever you need it. Even if you do it aloud, no one really pays attention or even cares. In time, as you achieve one success after another, those around you will take up the same habit. Winning is contagious.

Go for the little wins as well as the big ones. If every time you trim the bush in the front yard it looks like it has been mangled, learn to do it right. Work at it. Don't pass it off as unimportant. The first time it turns out evenly cropped, you'll feel as good as if you'd just won a race.

Learn how to manage your time. The lists you have made to plan your day should be reviewed each night. Carefully analyze why you didn't accomplish all you intended to that day. If the reason can be attributed to lack of time, start keeping a record of just how you are losing track of the hours. If interruptions are a problem, find a way around them. I wasn't kidding about my answering machine screening my calls. If you lose time in traffic, can your schedule be rearranged? If you spend too much time running errands, if they can't be eliminated, perhaps they can at least be combined. You can catch up on your reading by using cassette tapes of the books and listening to them on your walks. Getting more done in less time is like a puzzle. Make all the right pieces fit.

Congratulate yourself. Many times the only person who knows you've won is you. That's okay. You are the most important person. There's nothing wrong in acknowledging you've done well. Pride in accomplishment spurs on even greater effort. Give yourself a pat on the back. Give yourself two. Do it as often as you can. You deserve it.

♦

Controlling the Setbacks

Now that you're prepared to succeed, get ready for the setbacks. They're going to come.

When I came to the Chicago White Sox in 1973, they had a star already in place. His name early in his career was Richie Allen. Later he wanted to be known as Dick Allen. Whatever the case, Dick Allen could really play. In 1972 he hit 37 home runs and drove in 113 home runs.

To give you an idea of how talented and determined a player he really was, as a young man he suffered a tremendous hand injury and continued on, never letting it affect his goal of a major league career. And a hand injury is one of the most devastating injuries any player can have.

◆

As the story goes, and the story is always up for debate, he was pushing a car late one night, and his hand went through the headlight. What the injury left him with was the inability to feel in the last two fingers of his right hand, making it extremely difficult to grip a baseball. All hitters, especially before the advent of batting gloves, have batting blisters from holding the bat a certain way. On Dick's right hand, you can see two distinct batting blisters, one from before the accident, the other after he changed his grip.

Two stories about Dick Allen come into play. The first involves Mike Cuellar, who in 1973 was with the Baltimore Orioles. Dick said Cuellar always started him off with a big slow curveball. "If he starts me off with a big slow curveball tonight, I'm going to hit it over the roof in left field." This was old Comiskey Park and only seven or eight men had ever hit the ball over the roof in left field.

Sure enough, in the second inning when Dick Allen came to bat, Mike Cuellar started him off with a big slow curveball. And sure enough, Dick Allen hit the ball right over the roof. A monstrous shot and one that he had called ahead of time.

The second incident occurred in Milwaukee during one of my starting appearances in 1973. It was a very cold day in Milwaukee. With one out and a man on second in the sixth inning, a ground ball was hit to the first base side of the mound. The runner on second took off for third, as I threw to Dick at first base. Well Dick dropped the ball, making the batter safe, and the runner on third headed for home. Dick should have thrown the runner out at the plate, but the numbness in his hand caused him to throw wildly. By the time the whole thing was over the bases were cleared and the Brewers led two to nothing.

I was taken out after the seventh inning, but before I was taken out Dick Allen came up to me, looked me straight in the eye, and said, "I'll get them back for you."

In the eighth inning, with two outs, the Brewers walked a man ahead of Dick Allen. The wind was howling in from right field about twenty-five miles an hour as Dick stepped to the plate. He proceeded to hit a ball as hard as I've ever seen a man hit a baseball. It cut right through the wind in right field and landed in the seats. Dick had tied the game at two to two. On his way back, all he did was wink at me.

I was convinced that Dick Allen could do anything he wanted to do. No matter that he suffered the worst kind of injury an player can suffer, and not recover fully from it. Dick Allen turned what could have been a major setback into an obstacle. He evaluated his changed circumstance, found a way around the problem, and kept his focus on his goal. In this respect, I have never seen a man more adept at getting the job done.

At one point, I thought the most difficult thing in my life to accomplish would be making the major leagues. Once I got there, I found that making the majors was hard, but staying there was even harder.

Because of some injuries to my arm and my lack of concentration, my rookie year was not going well. Charlie Fox, manager for the Giants, and I were not getting along. The San Francisco Giants weren't on top of their game either. We had just come off a particularly difficult series of games, and the next series, against the Pirates, wasn't looking to promising. We got into Pittsburgh at three in the morning. I was wiped out.

As I got into the hotel lobby, Charlie Fox, called me over. "We're going to have to send you back to the minor leagues. We're going to have to make a change."

It was like someone had punched me in the stomach and knocked the wind out of me. This thing

♦

I had built my whole life around was being taken away. Charlie was telling me I wasn't good enough. Maybe he was right. Maybe I wasn't good enough to pitch. I had times of doubt in the past, but never had I come close to believing I didn't have the stuff. I always figured I'd find a way around the problem and get to pitch anyway. Going back to the minors was big time. Would I ever make it back?

Going back to the minors brought back a lot of feelings, feelings which I hadn't had since that summer I had to leave Cape Cod. I was angry at Charlie Fox and myself, but primarily at Charlie Fox. Being sent down to the minors bruised my ego, insulted my ability to play, and generally interfered with the goals I had set for myself. I was a good pitcher, certainly good enough to pitch for San Francisco. I felt as if all the Giants' problems were being placed on me.

However, back to the minors I went, in a frenzy to work my way back up, and quickly. The injuries I had suffered had healed and I worked at getting my arm into shape. I had the same determination as I had the summer and fall of 1969. My father's words kept coming back to me, "Once you get there talent wins out. But first you must get there."

Emotionally I was back to that batting practice in Casa Grande, where every day was my World Series, because once again it was. Slowly my skill regained the consistency I needed to keep on track. My concentration increased. I was becoming the player I should have been the first time out. I was no longer asking myself would I ever make it back. I now thought in terms of *when* I make it back.

And make it back I did. A short time after I was sent down, I was called back up. The rest of the season went reasonably well, although not great. I was still conscious of my injuries, although I worked around them. The Giants themselves were having a banner year, but I found myself performing to what I believed were their low expectations of me. I was back in the majors, though, doing my job.

While I was now concentrating better on my performance, I still hadn't found a way to deal with Charlie. I can't say we were at each others' throats day in and day out, but we certainly weren't a mutual admiration society. So, at the end of the 1971 season, Jerry Donovan, the general manager called me in and asked, "Steve, do you think you can get along with Charlie Fox?" I thought about it, in retrospect not long enough, and said, "I don't think so and I feel that it would be in my best interest if you can get something for me someplace else." That was the first of my trade demands and little did I realize there would be quite a few more before my career was over. Jerry said he'd see what he could do, but the Giants didn't trade me after that 1971 season.

At the end of the 1972 year, Jerry Donovan called me in again. "Steve, do you think you can get along with Charlie Fox?" This time I thought a little longer. "You know, I'm a year older, now, and I've learned what the major leagues is all about. Yeah, Jerry, I think I can get along with Charlie. I'd like to stay here in San Francisco, and I'd appreciate it if you didn't trade me." Jerry said he'd see what he could do.

Shortly after this conversation with Jerry, I was in Carmel, California, playing in a golf tournament. Hank Sauer, my booster from that first spring training camp and an avid golfer himself, was there also. After the tournament, we were having a drink together in the bar and Hank proceeded to tell me the story of my two years with San Francisco. "You know, *kid*," two and a half years later and he's still calling me kid, "they wanted to trade you after that first year, but I told them to keep you, that I thought you were going to be a good pitcher. During the course of this year, they talked about trading you, but I said keep this guy, because somewhere down the road, this guy's going

◆

to be able to pitch. Steve, I want you to know that as long as I'm with the Giants, you're going to be right here. I'm in your corner."

Little did I know, as he was making that speech, the Giants' organization was offering me to just about anybody who could come up with anything. As it turned out, ten days later, I was traded to the Chicago White Sox, along with Ken Henderson, for Tom Bradley. The long and short of it is that Hank Sauer is *still* with the San Francisco Giants organization, while I have been long gone, lo these many years.

Being confronted with a major setback can be devastating. It depends upon how sensitive a person you are and how much you have developed your mental toughness. There are those people who can do something, fail, and pick themselves right back up again as if nothing has happened. Those people are either highly disciplined and goal oriented or they are oblivious. Others take the first sign of rejection as a sign that every negative belief that has been inserted into their subconscious was true. This setback is just one more confirmation.

My feeling is that you have to be a pretty tough person to open yourself up to the possibility of complete failure, and tough enough to take it if this failure is only one in a series. On the other hand, if you never open yourself up to the possibility of failure, you never allow for the chance of success.

Life for those people who keep themselves closed is a lot less stressful. Expectations are most often met because the expectations of these people are generally low. Change is kept to a minimum. Those people guarantee disappointments are not overwhelming. They never have to come face to face with defeat. And that's one way to do it.

By insuring this comfort level, however, these people seldom experience the elation of success. They never know the sheer joy of seeing a job well done.

♦

They never know how good it feels to expend all their energy and take pride in the result.

For many years I took the safe route because I thought I would be better off safeguarding what I did have rather than going for the win. What good did it do me? In the long run, I was going to lose the very thing I was trying to protect.

By the end of my second year at ABC, I realized that they were very much linked into the "hot" broadcaster syndrome. They took me aboard because I was a Cy Young Award winner who happened to retire at the beginning of June, just in time to coincide with the start of "Monday Night Baseball." I learned very quickly that I could be replaced by the next "hot" prospect who came along. There was no doubt in my mind that the minute Jim Palmer retired, he'd be in and I'd be on my way out. As it turned out, when Earl Weaver retired, he wound up at ABC.

Added to ABC's focus on who was "hot" rather than cultivating loyalty with their employees, the relationship between Howard Cosell and I was degenerating. There were more incidents in which he sacrificed journalistic integrity to gratify his own ego. These were not only at my expense, but at the expense of whoever happened to be near. It was quite obvious, though, that ABC had a relationship with Howard they were not willing to give up. Al was wrong, there weren't three options in dealing with Howard. There were only two, do it his way or get out. Unconsciously, I was looking to get out.

As it happened, I had maintained many of my contacts in Chicago from my time there. I was involved with a group in the restaurant business. Even my dentist was in Chicago. We were scheduled to broadcast from Milwaukee, and my plan was to stop off in Chicago, take care of some business, then drive up to Milwaukee in time for the game. Providence was with me again.

◆

I was down at the newsstand at the Ambassador Hotel when a bellhop said to the lady behind the counter, "Two papers for Mr. Caray."

"Harry Caray?" I asked.

The bellhop wasn't about to tell me anything else, so I gave him my card with my room number written on the back. "If you would just give it to Mr. Caray, I'd appreciate it."

I was not back in my room more than five minutes when the phone rang. "What are you doing here?" It was Harry. Who could mistake that voice?

So I told him. "I'm going to get a haircut, see my dentist, and drive up to Milwaukee. We're doing the Brewers tonight."

"That's okay," he says. "But before you go, I want to tell you something. Remember awhile back I told you I wanted you to be my partner. Well, now we're looking for somebody. Don't leave your room." End of conversation.

I didn't know whether to expect a knock on the door or what, but minutes later the phone rang again. It was Jim Dowdle, president of Tribune Broadcasting. "We'd like to talk to you about the WGN job. Would you be interested in listening to us?"

Milo Hamilton, now broadcasting out of Houston, was Harry's partner and they got along like oil and water. Milo started out working with the Cubs organization as a partner to a gentleman by the name of Jack Brickhouse. The Wrigley people, who owned the Cubs at the time, had promised Milo the number one baseball job when it came time for Jack to move on. As a matter of fact, at the end of the 1981 season, there was kind of a ceremonial passing of the torch between Jack and Milo.

The problem arose between 1981 and 1982 when the Wrigley people sold the team to the Tribune group. They realized, and rightfully so, that if you don't have the best product in the world, you better go out and

♦

get yourself the best salesman. And there isn't a better salesman for baseball than Harry Caray.

The Tribune group lured Harry away from the White Sox, who he had been with for eleven years. They, too, had just gotten new owners, so the transition on that end was easy.

This made Milo the odd man out. But because Milo also did basketball and was a competent broadcaster, Harry was made the number one television man and Milo was given the number one radio job. That left a position open for a color analyst.

My father always told me to listen to what people have to say, what's the worst that can happen. I was getting paid by the Orioles for the next four years. ABC was paying me $4,000 a week. I was under no economic pressure to get a job. With ABC, I was working one day a week, not a bad schedule. So the thought of doing 150 games a year was a major consideration. Then I realized, if I was going to make TV a career, I better hone my skills, and what better way to do that than by working at it. Getting in there and just doing it. I didn't realize at the time how good the job was. All I knew was that I liked Chicago and I wanted out of ABC.

Very shortly into the job, I realized something I had never noticed before, even as a Cub player—the overpowering loyalty of the Cub fan. As a player, I knew we weren't very good, and I translated my dissatisfaction into a lower level of fan approval. Boy, was I wrong. Over the years, this Cub fanaticism has become stronger. In 1982, the Cubs went cable. Suddenly, this team with fervent regional appeal went national. Cubs fans came from all over. The Cubs grew bigger and I was grateful to be part of that growth.

I could have let my experience at ABC sour me on broadcasting as a career. If I had caused enough problems for Howard, he could have killed my chances right then. That didn't happen. ABC was not

♦

threatening my contract. Nobody at the network told me I was not going to do "Monday Night Baseball" any longer. A network job like that is not something one gives up without thought. Any number of negative outcomes could have developed, backing me into a corner, forcing a decision I may not have wanted to make. But they didn't.

By that time in my life, I had learned to listen to what my inner-self was telling me. For every advantage my situation held, there was something that nagged away, forcing me to question it. Howard was a stumbling block, but it's silly to assume you will get along with everybody anyplace you are. I managed for two years to keep my head above water with him, nothing led me to believe I couldn't continue to do so. It wasn't Howard. It wasn't the network. It wasn't the fear of being out and the new star being in. It was me.

We've seen the self-fulfilling prophecy of failure and we're surrounded by people who work against our success. Achievement is a constant battle. The only way we can keep on the right track is to recognize when we've gone off course and go back to the basics.

During the entire time I was starting my broadcast career, I was still heavily involved in the restaurant business. I still had goals to meet in that area, and the responsibility for ensuring others' success. The business was doing well. There wasn't a doubt in my mind that I could spend the rest of my life in the restaurant business and still not have the time to achieve all I wanted to.

I approached the WGN job with the same deliberation that I approached the Oakland A's game after the All-Star break. I visualized myself on "Monday Night Baseball." I saw myself in the booth, with all the great people I worked with, and the not-so-great. I let myself feel how it would be to continue on that course.

I envisioned myself in the restaurants. One of my favorite things had been development of new dishes. I must have come up with twenty new ways to do turkey. A great deal of satisfaction is gained when you watch people enjoy what you have prepared for them. I had to ask myself, "Is this enough?"

After all the time I had spent perfecting my meditative and visualization technique, I found that consciously going back to basics, step-by-step, finding my way through the maze of options, was the most successful for me. I rebuilt the positive cocoon, piece by piece. Not that I had developed any negative beliefs about what I could accomplish, I hadn't. What I wanted to do was reinforce my ability to keep my focus forward. I wanted to be stronger.

I cannot say it enough times. This process needs to be kept strong. It can't be used then put away until things have gotten so bad you realize you need it again. That's like losing fifty pounds then waiting until you gain back one hundred before you go on another diet.

It can't be done by rote. You will get to the point that you relax the moment you close your eyes. You will fall into a pattern of meditating on the same things. If you are not careful, you will lose the ability to see all the alternatives. Like everything else, this process reaches its own comfort level. Once that comfort level is reached, the same dangers inherent in other activities appear in this one.

By keeping yourself challenged, you will prepare yourself for those times when circumstances beyond your control throw up a blockade to your success. A good way to be ready for these obstacles is to visualize yourself in your current position, already having taken steps toward your goal. Visualize what can go wrong, even if there's only a million to one chance. After you've outlined all the possible blockades, build defenses against the blockades, or better yet, roadways around them. You're not caught off guard if they do occur, and you can respond immediately to any situation.

◆

Do not think that if you follow the steps I've outlined that every performance will be successful the first time and every goal will be met. That is fantasy and an excellent way to set yourself up to fail. Achievement is a series of trial and error, of disciplined determination. What you want to do is minimize the setbacks to your goal. You'll never totally eliminate them.

My restaurant, Steven, was successful; however, as time went on, tastes changed and the market was growing more towards a less formal more sports-oriented clientele. While I could have continued to run Steven profitably for many more years, I realized that the growth area for restaurant-bar operations was in the trend toward "sports bars."

I took stock of my positives. I knew the restaurant business and had developed a good reputation. I was also a personality in the sports industry. Put the two together, I was a natural. I also had another advantage, a great partner.

Like I said, Cub fever is nationwide, and one of the most fervent pockets of Chicago fans outside of the Midwest is in the Phoenix area. My partner in the booth became my partner in the restaurant business as well. What developed was Harry and Steve's, a sports bar in the Phoenix area. And it is doing very well.

I could have struggled to keep my original restaurant theme going and probably would have made it, but at what cost. I had to look at the goal.

I wanted to operate a successful restaurant, one which could grow within the market. I did not necessarily want to run a fine dining establishment. I took great pride in Steven, but I knew when it was time for a change.

I did not wait for the major setback to occur. I didn't have to lose money year after year. I didn't hold out until I saw something that I had made a success

◆

turn to failure. I evaluated the resources at my disposal, reassessed the goal, and changed the method of reaching this goal to accommodate them both.

Never rest on your laurels. Shake yourself up from time to time. Keep yourself in practice. Turn what could be a setback into a minor adjustment in your plan.

♦

Becoming a Tough Competitor

Now that we have the tools with which to win, the next step is to analyze the contest itself, study the method of encounter, learn how to compete.

There are those today who think that they can bury their heads in the sand and avoid competition, or those who speak out against the structure of competition itself likening it to a hostile adversarial position. The reality is that competition is adversarial, but it does not have to be hostile. There is a winner and a loser, but losing is not synonymous with devastation. And the very essence of competition is uplifting rather than demeaning as its critics would have you believe.

Each one of us competes every day. I'm not talking about the race to see who is first at the traffic light, or the person who wants always to be first in line in a store. We compete in healthier ways. Students compete to get into a good college by testing and interviewing well; athletes compete in whatever their particular sport is; we all compete on our jobs for the praise and ultimate rewards from those we work for. We judge others who compete for us. If we are in positions in our jobs which require us to hire others, we let those who seek employment with us compete and then we choose the winner. Teachers award students each day. Even our children compete for their own level of athletic reward, and we as their parents, judge their efforts.

The competition for what we have goes even further. We can't avoid it, it's all around us. Advertisers compete for our dollars; organizations compete for our time; issues compete for our attention. The act of competing permeates our lives and we must understand how it works, how to recognize it, how to evaluate its effectiveness, and, in the end, how to use it to our advantage.

Athletic competition allows us to compete in the purest form. Unlike life, which presents a lot of grey areas in the competitive processes, sporting competitions have a winner and a loser. Even as a child I was a very competitive person. With my involvement in athletics, very early on I developed the philosophy that if there was going to be a winner in any situation, there was no reason why the winner shouldn't be me. I find that true even today. I play racquetball, tennis, golf, and even bowl, on occasion. Although these are little competitions with no great reward hanging on the outcome, nothing of value on the line, I compete with the same fervor as I did when I was involved in the major leagues. My baseball career taught me how to recognize the flow of the competitive process and

◆

this knowledge has carried through even though I no longer play.

This brings me to one of the most important factors in the competitive process, and that is recognizing when, during the course of the significant event, the "critical" moment occurs. This critical moment is when the outcome of the situation is determined; it is the time when the resolution of the situation could go either way. And this moment comes at various times of the event, it's not always the last inning of a baseball game, or the last two minutes in football. It is not the final presentation during a sales call, nor is it the interview when your boss is determining who gets the promotion. This critical moment can happen any time. It is the winners who recognize when it occurs.

It is at this juncture that all your concentration must be focused on the task at hand. Intensity must be heightened or the opportunity will pass unexploited. I do not mean that before and after this critical time that all the forces you have learned to bring to bear on your success should be ignored, far from it. A vigilant performance at all times increases the likelihood that at the critical moment your behavior will be that most effective in reaching your goal.

Let me give an example from racquetball. You're playing a best two out of three match. You've won the first game; your opponent has won the second. You're playing to fifteen and in the third game you start and you're ahead by five points. Suddenly your opponent comes back and no longer are you ahead five to nothing, now he's ahead seven to five. He's got all the momentum going for him.

This is the critical moment, the moment in which you recognize that the momentum has left you and swung over to your opponent.

As a competitor, the first thing you have to do is break the momentum of your opponent. If you can do that, maybe, if he's not as strong minded as you are, you can break his concentration. Sporting events are a question of momentum and knowing when to stem the tide is essential to success. Coaches call a time-out. Jimmy Connors, who played top line tennis longer than just about anybody, took a little time to adjust the strings on his racket. The strings on his racket did not necessarily need adjusting, but this pause gave him time to psyche himself up, to raise the level of his game and, more importantly, time to halt his opponents momentum and maybe his concentration. This accomplished, Connors would move to throw his opponents rhythm off and change the rhythm of the match.

Which brings us to the rhythm of competition. Rhythm of competition is something you hear about from all sportscasters, and I myself use it to describe pitchers who have their good rhythm on one day or another. Others refer to it when talking about the serve in tennis. Or a bowlers release of the ball. A golf swing is an excellent example of rhythm. A perfectly executed golf swing looks like a one movement activity. Everything reacting as one, the legs of the golfer, the hands of the golfer going into the backswing and in the same motion turning the direction of the club into the swing itself, and the follow-through. As a competitor, you have to realize that you must do whatever it takes not only to maintain your own rhythm but break the rhythm of your opponent.

I understood the rhythm of my curveball and it was almost a counting situation for me. On the mound, if I took one step backwards and started in my motion, I would bring my leg up, the leg would come down, my hands would come through and the ball would be on its way. The activity had its own beat. I figured out just how many counts it took, attached these counts to all the separate movements, and established a rhythm of throwing the curveball.

♦

One—Two—Three—Four—Five. The first part of my motion was slow, the second part was a little faster. When I would get out of rhythm, when the curveball wasn't breaking the way I would like it to, I would go back to the counting system and mentally count off as I made my throw.

Every situation has its own rhythm. Maybe you find yourself speaking too fast as you become nervous. In an interview, this is easy to do. If you've visualized the situation, you've probably accounted for this possibility and come up with a way around it. Perhaps you have thought of a relevant question you could ask to make the interviewer the speaker, not yourself. As he responds to your question, maybe your rhythm recouping technique could be deep breaths, or an unobtrusive way of rubbing your hands together to bring your focus back on your own rhythm. Whatever it is, establish your own "beat" before you have to face a critical situation.

As far as baseball pitchers are concerned, there are many who have great rhythm, for a couple of innings, then they just seem to fall apart. Part of this is concentration, certainly, but a more important part is that they have not developed a method of getting that rhythm back. They don't know their game well enough. In your case, if this happens to you, perhaps you have not analyzed the situation as you should have.

As human beings, it is difficult for us to look in the mirror and evaluate ourselves personally, our strengths and weaknesses, our virtues and shortcomings. I think it is easier to see ourselves through our performance, standing back and watching ourselves go through our activities and observing as any outsider would. If we focus on evaluating our performance, then, we will be able to identify those areas within a situation in which our strengths lie and those areas of our greatest weaknesses. If we can do

♦

this, we can maneuver the situation such that our opponent will play to the area of our greatest strength. This is the thinking man's approach to competition, leaving as little as possible to chance.

As a pitcher throwing the fastball, my strength was throwing over the right side of the plate, outside to left-handers, inside to right-handers. I could do that fairly consistently. It was a little more difficult for me throwing the ball outside to right-handers and inside to left-handers. Recognizing my strengths and weaknesses, I had to work around what I knew I could do and what I knew I might not be able to do.

If a right-handed hitter was weak outside, that being my weakness, I wasn't going to go there first. I would go to my strength first. I didn't care what I knew about an opponent as far as the scouting report was concerned. I always played to my strength, I didn't play to his weakness. As a competitor, you will have to do the same thing, go to your strength first. If you are up against someone else for the job, you will be more successful in the interview telling the boss why you *can* do the job than explaining why your opponent *can't*.

In many cases you find that you are up against a competitor whose strengths are the same as yours. In those cases, what you need to do is devise an adjustment to your plan. In my case, if I was up against a right-handed hitter who was good inside, I would go outside with my curveball or my slider, which I could control better on the outside than my fastball. There is always an adjustment available to your plan, if you properly evaluate the situation.

There were two right-handed hitters in baseball who consistently hit me very well. There were a lot of left-handers who hit me very well, but the two right-handers were Jim Rice and Buddy Bell. Both of them had the same attributes as hitters, although Jim Rice had a lot more power. Jim Rice was a star for many years with the Boston Red Sox and Buddy Bell made his name with a lot of different teams over the years. I faced Buddy while he was with the Cleveland Indians and the Texas Rangers.

Both of these hitters were quick enough to deal with the fastball inside, but kept their hands back long enough to hit either my curveball or slider away. When I faced either of them, I had to go away from what I did best. Consequently, they hit me very well. They didn't always beat me, but they beat me quite a bit.

On the left-hand side of the ledger, those who hit me very well were Ted Simmons, both with the St. Louis Cardinals and later with the Milwaukee Brewers; Cecil Cooper, also with the Milwaukee Brewers; and George Brett, who won the batting title in 1990, giving him a batting title in three different decades.

In 1981, I was to be the opening day pitcher against the Kansas City Royals in Baltimore. My parents were in the stands and next to them Earl Weaver. I was warming up in the bullpen waiting for the presentation ceremony for my 1980 Cy Young Award planned for before the game. My parents were going to accept the award for me. Kansas City, as was tradition, was taking batting practice before the game.

As my parents and Earl were watching Kansas City, Earl turned to my parents, and, in his gravelly voice, said, "Hey, do you know who that guy is out there?" pointing to a left-handed hitter taking batting practice. My father and mother looked at each other quizzically and shook their head no at the same time.

"Well, that's George Brett," Earl continued and paused a minute for effect. "You know what he's hitting off your kid?" Earl didn't wait for an answer. "He's hitting .480 off your kid. Do you think your kid can strike this guy out?"

Obviously my father had no idea if I could strike George Brett out, but Earl did. Earl knew what every hitter was hitting off every pitcher and George Brett against me was no exception. That's one of the reasons Earl was as good a manager as he was. He knew everything about everybody as it related to their baseball performance. He left nothing to chance. If I had been in trouble late in the game and George Brett had been the next scheduled batter, Earl, knowing the stats, wouldn't have allowed me to face George. That had been the competitor in Earl Weaver, the fact that he knew on any given day he was better prepared to manage a baseball team than the manager he was going up against. Not only did Earl know how every hitter did against every pitcher, Earl knew how they did in specific innings. In baseball, it's important to know how a pitcher will respond in the first three, the middle three, and the last three innings. There's a lot of hitters that a pitcher will seem to get out the first couple of times up, but the third or fourth time up, the hitters gain the advantage.

As it turned out, George did hit a home run off me that day, but I wound up beating the Kansas City Royals.

Practice is essential to insuring a good performance, but practice for the sake of practice is useless. Being able to practice effectively is an art in itself. An example from golf: On the putting green, do you just scatter the balls and see which ones you can drop? Or do you visualize that you are really on the eighteenth green and this is the shot for the match? On the driving range, you shouldn't just hit five irons as far as you can straight to the yardage marker. You should hit five irons that you draw from right to left. You hit five irons that you fade from left to right. You punch a few 170 yards or so. You make that practice work for you.

Practice, to be effective, should be two things. First, it should be directed. What do you want to accomplish? What is the method by which you want to accomplish it? If you are preparing to give a speech, is this practice intended to test your memory? Or is it to develop the proper body motion for delivery? Are your practice serves in tennis supposed to train you to deliver an ace down the middle on a first serve or a powerful ball for a second serve down the outside line? Mindless activity produces undisciplined performance. So what if you can throw a baseball right over the plate every time? What do you do if you need to throw it outside?

The second direction of practice should be situational. Practice situations are stressless when compared to those times we are actually called upon to perform. No matter how well you punch that five iron on the driving range, if you don't visualize the two sand traps and the grass bunker it has to fly over, when you get to the real situation, you will be unprepared. Always create a mental stress situation to accompany the physical activity. For that speech, don't practice in your room alone, pretend your audience is already there. Look around the room, engage them in eye contact. When you finally get up to actually deliver the speech, you will find that you are not only prepared in respect to the words, you will be more comfortable in front of a crowd.

The situational focus of practice builds confidence, or what athletes refer to as being "tournament tough." This is the advantage you see that many veteran tennis players have over younger and possibly stronger and more talented players. The young ones can execute the shots, but not necessarily when faced with a high stress situation. It is the same advantage the older racquetball player we discussed earlier wanted to exploit.

In professional sports, this confidence leads to the ability to make the "big shot." We've all seen it, those guys who are able to make the great putt to win the tournament, or serve out the game with an ace. This confidence is more than the belief that an athlete is capable of making the shot. It approaches the absolute conviction some competitors have of knowing, without a doubt, that they can do what it takes to win. Michael Jordan, for example, in basketball. There's fifteen seconds left on the clock and the game is on the line. Michael Jordan *wants* the ball because he knows he can do it. On the reverse side, I've known baseball players, who, in the ninth inning with the game in the balance, pray that that ball doesn't come to them. In the seventh inning, they had no doubt they could catch that fly ball, but in the ninth, their belief changes. It shouldn't surprise you that these are the guys who invariably make the mistake that costs the game. Why? Because they do not have the confidence to compete.

I spoke earlier of Juan Marichal. In the latter part of the 1971 season, the San Francisco Giants had squandered a ten and one-half game lead down to a one-half game or a full game lead, depending on the day. We were in San Diego for the last game of the season, and the Dodgers were right on our tails. Juan told Charlie Fox, "Don't worry, just give me the ball. We'll win the game and take the division title." He was supremely confident in his ability to beat the Padres.

As it turned out, Willie Mays and Dave Kingman, who had just recently been called up, hit home runs that day. And Juan did just what he said he would. He defeated the San Diego Padres, opening the door for the San Francisco Giants to win the Western Division Championship.

At the time, I was too young in the world of baseball to apply Juan's confidence to my own performance but, in retrospect, Juan did what every great competitor does. He took the confidence he had in his own performance and translated it into the absolute knowledge that he would win the game.

It was in these situations, down to the wire, game on the line, that Thurman Munson shone. A lot of people talk about Reggie Jackson being Mr. October. And Reggie Jackson certainly had some great performances during the World Series and some great late season heroics for the New York Yankees. But ask any contemporary who played against Thurman Munson and Reggie Jackson at the same time, and almost without exception, they will tell you that Thurman Munson was the man you did not want to face in a clutch situation because Thurman Munson would find some way to come up with the big hit. That's a great reputation to have.

As I evaluate my career, especially my early years in the major leagues, I can see where my inability to take control of games in the late innings led right into the years I struggled with my performance. I can recall many games in those early years when I would pitch into the eighth or ninth inning, but invariably I would make a mistake that would wind up beating me. There was always that one bad pitch that would do me in.

One time that quickly comes to mind is a game I pitched against the Atlanta Braves. Tony Kubek was the color analyst for NBC on this particular Saturday afternoon. At the time the Braves had some good hitters in Hank Aaron, Ralph Garr, and a young Darrell Evans. Here I was a young pitcher going up against all this power. But by the end of the eighth inning it looked like I was going to shut out the Braves. I had completely handcuffed them all game long.

Atlanta also had a young guy on their team that year by the name of Earl Williams. I had faced Earl on several occasions during my time in the minor leagues and I knew Earl could not hit a breaking ball particularly well and he couldn't hit an inside fastball. Earl was a huge right-handed pull hitter, which meant that everything he hit would be to left field or left-center. I had him 0 and 2 with two men on and two outs in the ninth inning. At that point I told myself, "This guy can hit a home run. I can't let him hit a home run. Throw a high outside fastball as a waste pitch, and then come back with a curveball."

That was bad thinking on my part. Not only was the strategy wrong, but so was my attitude. I had introduced into my thinking the possibility that Earl could hit a home run off me. I also had sidetracked myself from the most direct route to a win by my plan to throw a waste pitch.

I threw the high outside fastball and, sure enough, Earl swung and he hit the only ball he hit off me to right field in his career. The ball went straight down the right field line and just over the fence. It was a three-run homer. The Braves beat me three to two.

I had been my own worst enemy. Not only had I put two men on base in front of Earl, but I psyched myself out to "not let this man get a home run," rather than planning to "get this man out with a curveball and be done with it."

I found out later that Tony Kubek had left the booth in the eighth inning and gone to the Giants' locker room. He was ready to interview the rookie pitcher who had defused the Atlanta Braves' power-house lineup.

This was not the only time I fell victim to the late inning home run. I can remember occasions when Rick Monday and also Ron Cey hit late inning home runs against me. My career is peppered with such incidents.

Of course, I wasn't the only pitcher this happened to. Bert Blyleven, a great pitcher, was also plagued early in his career by the same late inning failures. At one time it was said that if you could stay close to Bert during the course of the game, you could beat him with a late inning home run. For a starting pitcher, that kind of a tag is like a sentence to lose. Thoughts of a negative outcome are present even

◆

though there is no hint from the ongoing performance. These are the pitchers managers don't allow to
complete games. Fortunately for Bert, in later years,
he was able to get rid of that tag, but I am sure it was
not before he learned to allow his own confidence in
his performance to supersede any negative input
planted by past failures. I had to learn the same
lessons.

Getting beat in the late innings of a game was the
thing I most feared. To counter this fear, instead of
going right at the hitter with the understanding of
what it took to get him out, I would give myself a
negative thought almost excusing the possibility of
failure. I know now that I wasn't excusing failure, I
was insuring it. This is a key. Those things we are
afraid of the most, we dwell on the longest, thereby
increasing the likelihood that these things will indeed
come about. It's a vicious circle. The more we dwell on
these possibilities, the more often they occur, and
then the more we dwell on them.

A tennis player does not say to himself, "Okay, if
I miss the first serve, I'll give him a good kick serve on
the second serve." A successful competitor tells himself, "I'm one ace away from winning this match."

Remember when we spoke of that meeting with
your boss? Confrontation with anyone in authority
can be unnerving. After all, by definition, those who
have the authority over us control an aspect of our
lives, usually a critical one. When we are at the mercy
of someone else, there is fear. A natural emotion, of
course, but fear can cause us to perform less than
successfully. When you saw yourself speaking to your
boss, did you also see yourself relaxed? If you went
through the exercise several times, you probably did
and your behavior in your thoughts translated into
your actual behavior when you performed. The meditation was more than an intellectual exercise. It was
practice.

♦

Performing under pressure is an essential part of being a good competitor. Training your mind to accept the pressure and its accompanying distractions is critical to performing well. The only way to hone the skill of performing under pressure is to practice under simulated pressure situations.

Finally, the last piece in becoming a good competitor is realizing that the competition doesn't end. After you've reached that goal, or gotten that promotion, you must continually compete to maintain what you have accomplished. Even if your opponent is yourself and the standards you have to meet or beat are your own.

One of the things that comes to mind in my tenure as a Chicago Cubs broadcaster is the year Andre Dawson had in 1990. Here's a man who's had a series of serious knee operations. He came off a disastrous late season and playoff performance in 1989. Andre Dawson has always been a man who leads by example; he's not a rah-rah kind of guy, but the kind who goes out there day after day, the total embodiment of mental toughness. A lot of people felt that Andre's great years were left in Montreal before he came to the Chicago Cubs as a free agent. However, Andre proved them wrong. Look at his 1987 year when he won the MVP. But 1989 could have been the end. His knee problems had become extraordinary.

But before the 1990 season, while working out in Miami with Lenny Harris, a Los Angeles Dodger player, Andre made a prediction. Andre, coming off his injuries, told Lenny, "If I'm healthy this year, I'm going to win the MVP."

Andre did not win the MVP in 1990, but he put together a season that almost anyone would be envious of. He batted over .300, with more than twenty home runs. He became only the second man in the history of major league baseball to record over 2,000 hits, 300 home runs, 300 stolen bases in a career. All

◆

of this while running on a couple of knees which don't allow him many pain-free moments, on the field or off.

Watching Andre go out there day after day during the 1990 season is something I'll always remember. Often during the broadcasts it's hard for me to articulate just what a player goes through just to get on the field. I don't know how many more years Andre Dawson has or how effective he'll be over those years, but I do know the tremendous inner pride this man has made his great 1990 year possible. For Andre, the competition involved his being able to still give everything he's got.

The fortunes of the Cubs the last few years have revolved around the development of Jim Frey as both a manager and general manager. Jim Frey came from the Baltimore Orioles' organization where he was locked in as second banana behind Earl Weaver. During his tenure with the Orioles, Jim had his hand in just about every phase of the club, but because of Earl's position, he did not get the headlines or the credit he should have. Even after Jim took the Kansas City Royals to the World Series in 1980, he still never got the credit he deserved.

Jim Frey came to Chicago while Dallas Green was general manager, and, in 1984, Jim Frey got the Cubs to the playoffs only to fall short of the World Series. But, as so often happens to a manager whose team does not continue to find success, Jim was fired during the 1986 season with the Cubs in fifth place. But Jim bounced back and wound up in the WGN radio booth for the 1987 season.

Make no mistake, Jim's experience with the various ball clubs he had been associated with, both as a player and a manager, made him a valuable asset in the broadcasting area of baseball. He provided insight from all perspectives. However, Jim never lost the belief that he could contribute to a team's day-to-day success and operations. He succeeded as an an-

◆

nouncer, but kept his eye on the goal of getting back hands-on into the game. In 1987, Jim achieved what he wanted to achieve. He was back in the game as general manager of the Cubs.

When Jim came back it wasn't easy. His first trade was Lee Smith to the Boston Red Sox for Al Nipper and Calvin Schiraldi. Lee Smith was successful with the Sox and is still a top line reliever for the St. Louis Cardinals. Al Nipper and Calvin Schiraldi wound up doing nothing with the Cubs. Jim Frey took a lot of heat over that trade. Yet he didn't hesitate to make another controversial trade a year later. This trade, sending popular Rafael Palmeiro and four other players to the Texas Rangers for three players, one of which was Mitch Williams, brought the Cubs a division title in 1989. Rafael is a very good hitter, but the Cubs would not have won it in 1989 without Mitch Williams. Like any good executive, Jim Frey must make decisions, and live with those decisions, good or bad.

Jim Frey is a man who loves baseball. That was his goal, a career in the game. Early on, Jim realized that as a player he did not have the stuff to make his mark in the game. He reevaluated. As a manager he paid his dues. The manager's job is to win *this* year. With the Royals, he proved his stuff; in his managerial stint with the Cubs, he faced the harsh reality of failure. But this did not set him down. Keeping his hand in the game from the booth, Jim made adjustments to both his own skills and the perception others had of those skills. When he came back as general manager, he was able to link together his total experience in the game to provide the direction needed from the top.

A general manager must concern himself with the total organization, not just the players, but the whole staff, coaches, managers, secretaries, even the maintenance people on the field. These are the people who depend upon him for their livelihood. As a gen-

◆

eral manager, Jim is concerned with winning *this* year certainly, but he must look forward to the next year, and the year after that. He must concern himself with building a ballclub that will stand the test of time. As an executive, he cannot view his organization in terms of what it is today, but must make decisions as to what the organization will be tomorrow. Jim responds to these demands and is an excellent example of what a general manager must be to be successful.

Jim Frey's career in the game exemplifies a quality necessary to all successful competitors—flexibility—the ability to reassess any situation and react accordingly. This quality of flexibility hit home with me in 1987 when the Cubs organization suffered a tremendous shock.

In February 1987, Harry Caray suffered a stroke, which left everyone associated with Cubs baseball in any way, shape, or form anxious and distraught. The outpouring of cards and letters proved, in no uncertain terms, just how much Harry Caray was loved nationwide. Harry fought back like the trouper he is, but it was obvious to the Cubs organization and Harry that he would miss the beginning of the season. From his home in Palm Springs, Harry insisted he would make the booth by opening day; however, that was not to be. We all knew "the show must go on."

How to replace a legend? The executives at WGN finally decided not to replace Harry with one announcer, but, instead, to bring in a series of luminaries from all fields as guest hosts, one per day. The idea was that I would be the consistent presence in the booth to coordinate the broadcasts, but the guest would be able to select his own role. Each was given the choice of doing play-by-play, color, or just commentary. That left me to do whatever else was needed to keep the broadcasts going. Believe me, it was a unique experience in the annals of television and radio broadcasting, one which has not been duplicated.

♦

Brent Musburger, a consummate professional and an ex-Chicagoan with a good idea of what the Cubs and Wrigley Field are all about, was the first guest host. The broadcast was smooth and relaxed, Brent knowing what was expected of him and being able to cover the play-by-play with ease. For me, it was certainly not a portent of things to come.

My next guest was Mike Royko, as much a part of Chicago as the Cubs. Mike showed up exactly forty-five seconds before the broadcast. For the first time since the beginning of my broadcast career with the Cubs, I was nervous. I did not know what to expect. Added to the fact that Mike and I did not have a chance to talk before the game was that for the first time in my career, I was number one. With Harry, I followed his lead. This time I was in charge, a new challenge for me.

During the first break, I told Mike, "unlike writing a column, where you can start five or six times and if you don't like what you've said, you can ball it up and throw it into a wastebasket, every one of your mistakes goes out over the air. This is live television and you can't take back anything you've said." I may have overdone it when I told him "there is no safety net. There are no retakes to be shown on the 'bloopers' shows later on. This is it."

Mike is a wonderfully gifted writer. He has a way of stringing together words with meaning and humor; in his columns he speaks to the heart of the reader. That day, Mike seemed intimidated by live television.

My third guest was George Will, who I have come to respect both as a knowledgeable baseball fan and political thinker. George is on the board of directors of the Baltimore Orioles. He was well-prepared for the broadcast, as one would expect, and we were able to provide a conversational play-by-play which I appreciated. We have since developed a friendship from which I have benefited greatly.

♦

George Wendt, currently a star on "Cheers," and Danny Breen, of "Not Necessarily the News," were my next guests, and we were broadcasting from Philadelphia. These were interesting co-hosts, both being comedians, and George Wendt coming out of Second City, the improvisional comedy theater in Chicago.

Prior to the broadcast, we had been in the dining room, a room given to media people by every ballclub, so the staff from those organizations can get something to eat before the game. The food in Philadelphia is usually pretty decent, but that night they were serving little gray hamburgers. George did an entire act in the dining room over the burgers, pausing only to eat five or six of them.

Before we started, I explained to them that I needed one minute, forty seconds before the broadcast. "Just some sort of improv. Give me anything." Not too much to ask for, I thought, with the kind of experience these two guys had.

The broadcast starts, and I turn to them for their input, and what do I get—nothing. So I fill in. And I keep filling in. About an hour into the broadcast, I finally say to them, "Look, you have to give me something, anything."

"Like what?"

"Anything. How about the burgers. Talk about the burgers in the dining room."

George and Danny picked up on that and finally got into the spirit of the broadcast.

Bob Costas came along next and he was absolutely brilliant. He is a phenomenally gifted play-by-play broadcaster in whatever sport he chooses to do. This particular day, however, he was an extremely tired man, having been up most of the night before travelling.

Leon Durham, the Cubs first baseman, comes up in the ninth inning. The score is seven to six and there are two outs. Leon hits a towering home run. With that,

◆

Bob goes into his home run call, "It is a long drive. It's going. It's back. It's back. It's outta here. It ties the game at eight to eight."

I said, "Excuse me, Bob, that might have been a long home run, but it only tied the game at seven to seven."

At no other time have I seen Bob Costas make a mistake on television. But, being the consummate professional, he replied with one of the greatest comeback lines I've heard. "I thought I was coming here to replace Harry Caray. Instead, I came here to commit hara-kiri."

Improvisationaly, Bob's as good as they come.

Next came Ernie Harwell, who spent more years than I can count with the Detroit Tigers. When he stepped in the booth, it was as if the old war-horse had come to the stage. The broadcast went smoothly. Ernie seemed to just open his mouth and the words came tumbling out. It didn't matter that he was not familiar with the league, just watching the Hall of Famer was a thrill.

Pat Summerall was my next broadcast partner. As a football broadcaster with CBS, Pat is low-key, playing off his partner, John Madden. They make a wonderful pair. As a baseball broadcaster, however, I don't think Pat was as comfortable as he might have been. He didn't say much as the game went on, making the broadcast not necessarily bad, but difficult.

Skip Caray, Harry's son, was a pleasure to work with. As the broadcaster for the Atlanta Braves he has an irreverent sense of humor and carries on the Caray tradition of a love of baseball. Pinch-hitting for his father, I think, was something special for Skip. For me, it is interesting to have worked with both the senior and junior editions of the same family. Perhaps some day I will be fortunate enough to work with the third generation, Chip Caray, Skip's son, who now does basketball for the Orlando Magic.

◆

My next guest provided the wildest of all the broadcasts and one which will go down in the annals of the Cubs. Bill Murray gave Chicago a roaring good time.

Unlike those who have problems with unscripted material, Bill thrives on those situations. He is a genuinely funny man, and, perhaps, a genuinely crazy man. He was hysterical—Bill's mind works in ways most of us do not understand. Talk about irreverency. He picked on everybody, even his mother.

Once the game had started, Bill made a big deal about not being able to spot his mother in the stands, as if anyone could spot any one person in crowded Wrigley Field. After a while, when he still hadn't found her, he accused her of hiding from him. "She's out there drinking with the guys in the stands. Oh, come on in, Mom." Well, this went on and on, and the longer it continued the funnier it got, and the funnier it got the more difficult it was to concentrate on the game. I felt like I was part of the Bill Murray Show.

Finally, much to my relief, Mom shows up. Bill welcomes her like the prodigal parent. She did not deny it when I asked her if Bill was raised by wolves.

Bill is a baseball fan and extremely knowledgeable about the game. I understand he is involved in the ownership of the Salt Lake City Trappers, a minor league team. Because of his knowledge, I had an easy time of the broadcast, at least when I managed to maintain control of it.

This is still a broadcast that people want to see. WGN still has the tape and it is much in demand.

Bob Sirott was my next guest. Bob had done some television in Chicago and was, of late, on "West 57th." He, at one point, had aspirations of being a baseball play-by-play man and had come into the booth loaded for bear. I think it was his own audition.

He found out that play-by-play was not as easy to do as he thought it was. People who do it well, like Harry, like Bob Costas, make it sound a lot easier than

♦

it really is. To Bob's credit, he had a plan for the broadcast, he knew the direction he wanted to go. He did a good job and seemed to really enjoy himself. At one point, he admitted doing Cubs baseball was one of his lifelong dreams and he was glad to have his chance, even if it was only for one day.

A Hall of Famer and onetime partner of Harry Caray when Harry was with St. Louis, Jack Buck, followed Bob. Jack has got a great voice and a great delivery. Working with Jack was similar to working with Ernie Harwell, having some of the history of the game in the booth. The same thing holds true for the broadcasts I did with both Mike Shannon and Ken Wilson, other members of the St. Louis broadcasting team. They are a group of highly trained professionals whose knowledge of the game only added to the enjoyment of working with them. Since we were all baseball broadcast professionals we knew what to expect from each other. Gary Bender and Ron Rappaport were a pleasure, too.

Tom Bosley, who played the father on "Happy Days" and is also a lifelong Cub fan, came in very well prepared. He was definitive in his desire to do the play-by-play and we accommodated him.

Part of the texture of the Cubs' broadcasts is to make note on the air of those sponsors and luminaries who happen to send notes to the booth. In those days, there was a cigar sponsor on the radio who always used to stop by the booth. The day Tom did the broadcast, this sponsor came by, left a card, and gave cigars to all the people in the radio booth and to me, knowing that I was a cigar smoker. While on the air, we made mention of the sponsor and Tom said, "Oh, now I know where you get your free cigars."

Jack Brickhouse, another Hall of Fame broadcaster and a legend in Chicago, broadcast the Cubs for over forty years without ever broadcasting a winner. Jack is one of those people that everybody likes. He is

◆

prominent in Chicago society and active in the various charity events around town. I think Jack spends half of his life in a tuxedo. Having Jack in the booth was a wonderful experience. The Chicago fans love to see and hear him.

Jim Kaat, who later went on to work for ESPN and now CBS, is a very knowledgeable broadcaster. At that point, he was working the College World Series on a regular basis. As a left-handed pitcher, he won close to 300 games in the major leagues. His success has continued into the broadcast booth.

Steve Daley, a television critic for the *Chicago Tribune*, had an interesting broadcast. Steve didn't really know a great deal about broadcasting and he seemed a little intimidated by the microphone. Had he known how the broadcast was going to go, he might not have come down to the booth at all.

On this particular day, I wasn't feeling very well. Understand that I had never missed a game due to illness during my tenure with the WGN organization, and I wasn't about to miss this day. The pattern for the guest broadcasts involved the celebrity doing the first three innings with me in the television booth, then the guest would go over to the radio room for the next three innings, and in the seventh, the guest would return to me.

The game opened, I introduced Steve, and things went along as well as could be expected. At the top of the fourth, Steve moved over to the radio booth as scheduled and returned to work with me for the seventh inning.

As the game was progressing, so was my illness. I was becoming dizzier and dizzier, I was cold and hot at the same time, and my stomach was in knots.

We got to the bottom of the seventh inning and I said to Steve, "You better take the microphone over. Talk about whatever you can."

He turned almost as white a shade as I was.

◆

Finally, my stomach erupted and I buried my head in a wastebasket in the corner of the booth. Poor Steve Daley, who had not broadcast much, was trying to hold the ship.

When I felt good enough to lift my head, I managed to find my way into the other room and get Lou Boudreau, Hall of Fame player who was working on radio, to come and take over.

To the credit of both Lou and Steve, I don't think that the audience was really aware of what was going on. But the look of sheer terror in Steve Daley's eyes is one of my most vivid memories.

Dick Stockton, another seasoned veteran, is a fine broadcaster. His experience in the field made our teaming a real pleasure.

Ernie Banks is as beloved a Cub figure as there is. When the Cubs didn't have a whole lot, they had Ernie Banks. He took the sting out of a lot of last place finishes. Ernie was the first National Leaguer to win back-to-back MVP awards. He was the Cubs in those days and the Chicago fans today still remember. Like with the other Cub greats who guested, his presence added meaning to the show. The one thing that has remained constant since the first time Ernie Banks donned a Cub uniform is his love for the team. That love is certainly returned.

I did the next show from Los Angeles with Dennis Franz, Detective Norman Buntz first of "Hill Street Blues" and later on his own show "Beverly Hills Buntz." Dennis is a consummate actor, who, unfortunately, knows very little about baseball. As a matter of fact, in fourteen years in Los Angeles, Dennis has been to one Dodger game. He didn't know anybody on the Cubs team. The closest thing to experience in the game he had was the fact that he played a little baseball in high school. That was a tough broadcast, six innings of tiptoeing through the tulips.

Dennis is a wonderful man, and one of the nicest

guests on the broadcasts, but it was an uncomfortable experience for the both of us.

Harry Kalas has one of the great voices around. He is the Philadelphia Phillies broadcaster and also does some work with the NFL. This was an easy broadcast.

Jim Belushi was an interesting broadcast. Jim is a Chicago guy, and, if you've ever seen any of his work, there's always a Cubs' hat or t-shirt around. He's a great booster of the area. We did the broadcast from San Diego.

Like Bill Murray, Jim has his own unique personality. He is a funny man and a fine actor. There was an uncomfortable moment early on in the show when Jim made a comment which might have been misunderstood. I pulled back from that quickly. The WGN organization is very conservative station.

Overall, it was pretty good broadcast, not as funny as the Murray show, but it had its moments.

Duke Snider, a Hall of Famer who played with the Brooklyn Dodgers, was doing the Montreal Expos broadcasts at the time he guested on the show. Dick Enberg was another good broadcast. If you've ever watched Dick on television, you know that there is nothing Dick can't do behind the microphone. He's been broadcaster of the year a couple of times.

Tom Dreesen is always enjoyable. He is an excellent stand-up comic with strong roots in improvisational comedy. Anyone who has guested more than fifty times on "The Tonight Show" is most certainly talented. Once a year, for a week period, Tom is the Cubs' bat boy, probably the oldest bat boy in "batboydom." So it was only natural that we have Tom in for one of the broadcasts. Tom dressed in one of the old style Cubs uniforms and the fans loved it. He gave them a great show.

My friend Joe Torre, then a broadcaster, now the St. Louis Cardinals manager, came next, followed by Jay Johnstone, a former Cub and White Sox player who is always a lunatic. Jay has become a successful author and has since made a name for himself in broadcasting. I think this broadcast helped Jay get over the top in this phase of his career.

Pat Williams, general manager of the Orlando Magic basketball team, came into the booth with at least four games worth of material. He was one of the most prepared men I have ever seen. This quality certainly shows itself in his career as an executive in basketball. I was sorry that we didn't have seventy-five innings so he could use all of the anecdotes and research he had brought with him.He could probably do a show right now just from the notes he had leftover from that day.

The last man to guest was Bob Starr, broadcaster for the California Angels. Bob is a capable professional who made the show go smoothly.

Then the parade of celebrities came to an end. On May 19, 1987, Harry was well enough to come back.

I was thankful and relieved. Thankful because my friend had recovered well enough to return to doing what he loved best. Relieved because the trauma of guest celebrities was over.

I had visited Harry in March 1987, in his home in Palm Springs. At the time, the damage from the stroke had left Harry physically weak and unable to speak in the distinctive manner Cub fans had come to expect. I wondered if he would ever be able to return to the booth. I shouldn't have. Harry's strength of will and his love of the game made for a quick recovery by every standard, except for Harry's, of course.

For me, the challenge in the booth during Harry's absence will not soon be forgotten. If I ever had any doubts as to my ability as a play-by-play man, they are gone. Because I had evaluated the situation and measured the possibilities each broadcast offered, I was able to build on the strengths of my guests, as well as

◆

adjust to their weaknesses. It was my chance to expand my own performance as a broadcaster and enhance others' perception of my skill in that field. An opportunity opened up for me during this time, and my experience as a broadcaster coupled with my goal to be the best broadcaster I can possibly be, allowed me to capitalize on it.

When Harry returned to the booth, it was the most emotional day in Cubs' history. If Harry had any doubts how loved he was, he could have them no longer. The crowd came unglued. He was coming back to the ballpark. He was still their Harry. Thank God.

Anybody but Harry might have let the excitement of the fans overshadow the business of broadcasting that first day back. But Harry was not going to let anyone or anything interfere with the business at hand. Not even the president.

President Ronald Reagan was one of the thousands of well-wishers who welcomed Harry back. It was a great thrill to have the president call the booth during the middle of the broadcast just to let Harry know that his return to the microphone was important to everyone connected with the sport. The president had finished up his welcome and was just starting an anecdote about his wife, Nancy, and her ties to the Chicago and Illinois area, when Harry interrupted. "Excuse me, Mr. President, I have to be going now. Bobby Dernier just bunted for a base hit and we've got to get back to baseball." Then Harry hung up the phone. He may be the only man to ever hang up on the president on national television.

Some time later, though, President Reagan proved he was as much a trouper as Harry, when he stopped into Wrigley Field and did a couple of innings with Harry and me. It is one of my most memorable experiences.

That six week period in 1987 was one of the most exciting in my broadcast career. As exciting as it

◆

might have been though, during the time Harry was recuperating, I was back to competing as a broadcaster once again. No matter that I had many successful years as Harry's color commentator. We all know that years of success are quickly erased by moments of failure. I had to understand the new rules of the game and I had to play the game as well as I ever had.

The critical moment during this time was the broadcast itself. WGN Cubs baseball has a feel and rhythm determined by Harry's personality and the expectations of the fans. I had to deliver as suitable an alternative to both as I was able to do and, at the same time, maintain the technical integrity of the broadcast itself. No mean feat when dealing with the diverse personalities and talents who filled in for Harry during his absence. What made me ready for the situation was my understanding of it.

Just as I was prepared for the new circumstances, so should you be. Whatever your goal, the situation will never remain constant. Knowing how to compete is as important to winning as any other factor.

◆

What Others Teach

When is enough enough?

I've talked about the influence of my parents on my life and career. Between the athleticism imparted to me by my mother and the positive attitude consistently reinforced by my father, I was blessed with a winning combination to start with. To this I added my own desire and intensity and created an overachiever in athletics as well as in the worlds of business and television.

Besides my parents, though, four other men have helped me take a different view of life and showed me how to attain the goals and success I desired.

The first, Mel Korey, a native Chicagoan transplanted to Phoenix, is an example of someone who bounced around from career to career until the right one came along. Having lost both parents at a relatively young age, he was forced to raise his younger brother. There wasn't much money and times were tough, but they survived.

For a while, Mel ran a restaurant. Then he started a small vending company. That enterprise ended because he was at the wrong place at the wrong time competing against the wrong people, and his cigarette machines wound up on the sidewalk outside of some neighborhood bars. He even became a nightclub singer for a short time. Mel was gifted with intelligence and business sense, if not a lot of luck.

Then he teamed with Ron Popeil, a classmate of his from the University of Illinois. Millions of Veg-A-Matics, rhinestone stud setters, and stockings guaranteed-not-to-run later, Mel found success. He always said, "When you're panned by Dan Aykroyd of 'Saturday Night Live,' you know you've made it." Made it he did, Ronco was the king of the gadget business.

Mel didn't become a success by accident. He visited as many as fifty-five county fairs in forty-five days in twenty states with his Veg-A-Matic. He sold the thing to anyone who would listen. When he realized television was the county fair of the future, he became a telemarketer. Ronco had a long run, but when it ended, Mel took his telemarketing skills and parlayed them into a highly successful advertising agency.

Mel Korey will be successful at anything he choses. When you combine hard work, planning, a strong game plan, and the belief that you can do it, there's no way to fail. As a matter of fact, Mel's telemarketing techniques are now copied nationwide. Just look at the Home Shopping Network.

As Mel's friend I have seen how the natural insecurities that career changes normally bring were

♦

wiped away by Mel's strong self-belief. Mel can change course in midstream without breaking stride. Knowing Mel has taught me a good lesson. Like buildings need a strong foundation to withstand the capriciousness of nature, so people need strong foundations to hold up through the setbacks and the curves that life brings. Self-belief and confidence are the foundations that breed success.

The second major influence in my life was Rich Melman, the president and creator of Lettuce Entertain You Enterprises. Rich came from a restaurant background. His father owned a deli in suburban Chicago. As a young man, Rich wasn't academically motivated; college was definitely not in his game plan. Corned beef and chopped liver soon became his life. In time, Rich spun off from his father and started a Near North restaurant called R. J. Grunts. It became Jerry Orzoff, Rich's best friend and partner, and Rich against the Chicago restaurant establishment. In 1970, extensive salad bars, eclectic menus, and young, energetic servers were not the norm. For five weeks, nobody came to R. J. Grunts. Working on limited funds, Rich soon had his back against the wall.

One day, Rich left the restaurant to drive around the city of Chicago and evaluate his options. What wasn't he doing that he could be? Failure and its ramificatons were not a pretty picture. When Rich finally returned to the restaurant, there was a line waiting to get in. Twenty-one years and thirty some odd restaurants later, they're still waiting at Richard Melman's restaurants.

What does Rich Melman have that so many others don't? He doesn't *think* he's a great restauranteur. He doesn't *think* each and every business he'll develop will be successful. He *knows* he's a winner.

He has worked very hard and continues to outwork just about everyone I know. That in itself is not

♦

enough. He knows that belief builds confidence and confidence builds success. He can look at a vacant space and envision what it should look like, what it should feel like. He seems to know what people want before they want it. He's had a string of successful places that match or surpass every restauranteur in the country.

Richard has a formula for success, and I'm sure one day he'll share it in his own book. I know, though, that his formula is based on an inner and very real belief that he will make the right decision. You can't consistently choose the right and most successful projects without that strong self-image and confidence. It's a Catch-22. You can't be successful without a good self-image and a good self-image comes from success.

Turning inside ourselves is the solution to this Catch-22. We've outlined how you can reach inside yourself and pull out the intangible tools you need to do the job. Rich Melman found a way to bring out all the restaurant genius he had inside.

I've been a partner with Rich since 1974 and I've seen him grow from a small restaurant owner to one of the country's most respected and creative businessmen. He knows he can do it each and every time. And in the deli business from which he came, that ain't chopped liver.

The third great influence on my life is Harry Caray. Harry grew up as an orphan and he grew up in some very tough times. I remember the story he tells of not having the proper pants at his graduation and of how he decided at that time that as he grew up, he would be successful in life, and always have the proper pants for the occasion.

Harry knew that watching baseball games was very exciting and yet listening to the old St. Louis games on the radio never conveyed that excitement. He set out to tell the gentleman who was in charge of

♦

the broadcast that it could be done better than it was being done. Harry wrote a personal letter to this man and sent it to his home, knowing that it would get his personal attention. Had he gone through proper channels, that letter would have gotten lost in the shuffle. At that point, Harry was taking things into his own hands, in his own inimitable style.

The suggestion came back that Harry start off in some smaller markets, work his way up, etc., etc. But eventually Harry did do the broadcasts for the St. Louis Cardinals, and his enthusiasm and love of the sport bred a whole generation of Harry fans, and that enthusiasm is still evident today.

Another good example of how determined Harry is can be seen in the way Harry came to the Chicago Cubs. As I said earlier, the Chicago White Sox had a change of ownership about the same time as the Tribune Company was buying the Chicago Cubs. Once again Harry decided he was not going to sit back and accept the buffeting of life. He called Andy McKenna, the chairman of the board of the Chicago Cubs. He said, "Andy, I'm surprised at you."

"Why, Harry?"

"Because," Harry told him, "you haven't offered me a job yet."

"But I thought you were employed by the Chicago White Sox."

"No," Harry said, "I'm in the last year of my contract. I'm a free agent."

The rest is history. Instead of being a lovable local broadcaster, Harry has become a national cult hero. He goes into 22 million homes each time the Cubs play. When Harry Caray stands up during the seventh inning stretch, he commands the attention of the entire field. When he sings "Take Me Out to the Ball Game," the nation sings with him.

Harry Caray attacks life, make no mistake about it. Harry treats life strictly on his own terms. I've

♦

never seen a man who gets more out of every day. This man does what he wants to do just about 100 percent of the time and lives every minute that he's awake.

Being Harry's partner for eight years and watching him relate to the public, a couple of things pop out at me. Number one, he's the toughest man alive and absolutely fearless. I've seen him get off a bus in New York City at 3:00 A.M. and walk down the street, alone, looking for something to do. His stroke a few years ago certainly set him back a little, but it didn't stop him. A fitting epitaph for Harry Caray would be "Harry Lived."

The fourth great influence in my life was Bill Veeck. There was a lot of controversy as to whether Bill Veeck should be in the Baseball Hall of Fame. In my mind, if Bill Veeck was not in the Hall of Fame, then there should have been no Hall of Fame. It was a great pleasure to hear of his induction. I've never met a more progressive thinking, smarter, creative baseball man. He was the master showman, one of the most innovative men I've ever seen. I read an article Bill wrote several years before he died, in which Bill described for all of us what the sport would be like in the twenty-first century. His ability to look ahead was brilliant.

My roots with Bill go back much farther than the 1977 season when he hired me for the Chicago White Sox. On July 13, 1947, my very pregnant mother was walking out the door of her apartment. My grandfather called after her, "Where are you going?"

"To the ballpark," she said. "If I give birth at the park, maybe Bill Veeck will give me and my child lifetime passes."

As it turned out, she went to the park one day early.

Bill Veeck was one of the few men around who empathized with players who were less than 100 percent physically. This was because Bill went through a series of thirty-five or thirty-six major

◆

187

operations in his lifetime. He had a wooden leg and he was forever going into the hospital for one thing or another. Yet, I never saw a man with greater spirit and love for life, or with a greater understanding of how baseball worked and how to work within its framework. And he had to. Bill had to work within a system in which most of the owners had more money than he did. Bill always worked on a shoestring budget. Even with that, Bill Veeck put together an almost-division-winning team in the 1977 "Southside Hitmen."

Although pitching was artistic and pitching was effective, Bill realized that what put most people in the stands was excitement. Nothing builds excitement like a slugger. And Bill needed those people in the stands. He may have loved the game, but even he had to make a profit.

The 1977 Southside Hitmen had nine players that hit at least ten home runs. Some of standouts of that year were Oscar Gamble, who hit thirty-one home runs; Richie Zisk, who hit thirty home runs; and third baseman Eric Soderholm, who hit twenty-five home runs. We had Chet Lemon, who still plays for the Detroit Tigers, in center field, and Ralph Garr in left field. Throw in Jim Spencer with eighteen home runs, Lamar Johnson, who also whacked eighteen home runs, and Jorge Orta with eleven home runs and you had some real heat on the field. Catchers Jim Essian, with ten home runs, and Brian Downing, who is still playing for the California Angels, only added to the sheer hitting power of that 1977 White Sox team. We had a bunch of guys who could hit the ball very hard. Very few of the guys could catch the ball, but we caused excitement.

If the team didn't excite the crowd, the promotions would. Every day was some sort of day at Comiskey Park. Beer keg stacking day. Red, white, and blue day. Kid day. Hot dog day. Bring your dog day. Don't bring your dog day. There was a parade every day. People had a good time because Bill Veeck realized that having fun was what coming to the park was all about.

It was Bill Veeck, when he was with the St. Louis Browns, who sent a midget, Eddie Gaedel, up to bat. Naturally, he drew a walk. In his book, Bill said that he threatened to kill Eddie if he swung the bat.

Bill Veeck was as accessible as any owner has ever been. There was an area in old Comiskey Park called the Bard's Room where Bill set up a table with a telephone. Everyday, anyone associated with the park could come up to him and talk about baseball. He wanted to know what was going on in everyone's mind.

There was a method to Bill's madness. Like I said, Bill never had much money. He felt that there were a lot of players, who, though injured, still had the heart to give the game their all. Since many of them, like myself, came over as relatively inexpensive free agents, Bill could build on the strengths of these guys without spending too much money. It worked.

The game is diminished by his loss.

What do these four men have in common?

First, they all grew up with very little and were forced to make of life what they would with nothing but their own resources. Second, they each had an unshakable belief in their own ability to control their destiny. And lastly, each one of them approached each day with a new enthusiasm, an optimism that *this* day could be the best of their entire life.

Their positive attitudes have influenced me. Knowing them has given me a firmer commitment to my own goals because through them I can see that a strong self-belief, coupled with hard work, can bring about great things. To a man, they exhibit loyalty to their friends and employees, a belief that the world is open to those who put forth the effort to seize the opportunity, and confidence that the higher they strive, the more they will achieve.

◆

189

Just as these men have known success, so can you. The tools they used to reach their goals are the same tools that you already possess. Through meditation and visualization, you can use your own tools to build the commitment and confidence to seek out your own way. Whatever your goal, you can achieve it. It may not be easy, but step-by-step, it can be reached. Once there, you can achieve another goal, and another. You have no limits.

I have always felt no more than 25 percent of any athletic competition is physical. The balance is mental. As early as the late seventies, I was promoting the idea that teams—baseball, basketball, whatever—hire "mental" trainers as well as the physical trainers already on staff. As time has gone on, many have, but many more have yet to recognize the importance of that confidence which insures success.

I am reminded of an incident between myself and Maury Wills. After having won the Cy Young Award, I was very vocal in my interviews about the effect my mental retraining had on my achievement. I took care to outline the failures in my past record which led to my success during the 1979 and 1980 seasons. I wanted to show how this system did more for my evolution as a player than any of the physical programs I had been involved with. Maury had evidently paid a great deal of attention to what I was saying.

Maury himself was an interesting character. At the time of this incident he was manager of the Seattle Mariners. Bear in mind that Maury was not a particularly good manager, but as a player, he had shown brilliance. Until Lou Brock came along, Maury held all sorts of base-stealing records. After a long struggle, almost ten years in the minor leagues, Maury finally made it to the majors with the Los Angeles Dodgers. He then preceded to revolutionize the game of baseball. Before Maury Wills, you didn't have players who could steal bases at will. He was the

♦

forerunner to players like Lou Brock and Rickey Henderson, guys who combine great offensive skills with an ability to run. I think he saw in what I was saying the same things he instinctively knew as a player.

Maury invited me into the Mariners locker room to speak to the pitchers and catchers. He felt that what I had been saying in the various articles was something that could be of benefit to every player. What he wanted me to do was share some of this with the Mariners team. The situation was a little strange, of course. Not often does a player of the opposing team get invited to give a motivational talk before the game. However, at that point, I felt that sharing the system, helping other players, was something that needed to be done.

In 1985, when Dallas Green was the general manager of the Chicago Cubs and I was a broadcaster, the Chicago Cubs pitching staff was going through some tough times. I went to Dallas Green and Jim Frey, then the manager, and asked them if they would mind if I went down and talked to the pitching staff. I thought that by sharing my experiences back in 1979 and 1980, I would be able to help some of the pitchers improve their performances. Neither Dallas nor Jim had a problem with the idea, so speak to the staff I did.

In both of these cases, I got the feeling that, although some of the players knew what I was talking about, the mental commitment to take the system that had been so successful for me and incorporate it into their own performance was lacking. Perhaps there was even resentment. As a former player I knew it was hard to relate to someone outside my own team. I can't say whether either of these incidents actually made a difference in anyone's performance. The Seattle Mariners are still struggling to make their mark, and 1985 was not a banner year for the Cubs. So I was faced with a dilemma. How could I impart a system to

◆

improve performance that I know works, without having the listener immediately shut out the information because of some outside factor?

There it was, another goal, *to effectively communicate the process whereby anybody can achieve whatever goal they choose.*

So I ask you. When is enough enough?

Never.

Appendix

Steve Stone's Career Statistics

	G	GS	W-L	PCT	CG	SHO	IP	H	SO	BB	SV	ERA
1971 (SF)	24	19	5–9	.357	2	2	111	110	63	55	0	4.14
1972	27	16	6–8	.429	4	1	124	97	85	49	0	2.98
1973 (CHI-AL)	36	22	6–11	.353	3	0	176	163	138	82	1	4.24
1974 (CHI-NL)	38	23	8–6	.571	1	0	170	185	90	64	0	4.13
1975	33	32	12–8	.600	6	1	214	198	139	80	0	3.95
1976	17	15	3–6	.333	1	1	75	70	33	21	0	4.08
1977 (CHI-AL)	31	31	15–12	.556	8	0	207	228	124	80	0	4.52
1978	30	30	12–12	.500	6	1	212	196	118	84	0	4.37
1979 (BALT)	32	32	11–7	.611	3	0	186	173	96	73	0	3.77
1980 **Cy Young Award Winner**	37	37	25–7	.781	9	1	251	224	149	101	0	3.23
1981	15	12	4–7	.364	0	0	63	63	30	27	0	4.57
1982	Did Not Pitch—Voluntarily Retired											
	320	269	107–93	.535	43	7	1789	1707	1065	716	1	3.96

Index

◆